# The Pre-Tribulati

CW01511870

## by Derek Walker

(c) Copyright 2020 Derek Walker

www.oxfordbiblechurch.co.uk

# INDEX

**\*Cover Picture – The Morning Star just before Sunrise.**

The Morning Star is one of the beautiful pictures of the Rapture in the Bible (see Chapter 4). It appears while the world is still in darkness and is a sign in the sky heralding the soon appearing of the sun, when it will rise and cover the earth with its glory. Likewise Jesus is our bright Morning Star (Revelation 22:16), who will appear to His own and give Himself fully to them, but not to the world (Revelation 2:28), so that He will arise in their hearts (1Peter 1:19), releasing His glory within them and transform their bodies. This manifestation of Jesus in the Rapture, catching away His believers, will be a great Sign, heralding the soon Appearing of Christ in His Second Coming as the Sun of Righteousness, who will fill the earth with glory and bring in a brand new day of history – the Millennial Day of the Lord.

# *Foreword by Christine Darg

From my childhood I have experienced dreams about the Rapture even before I knew the name of the doctrine, which is found in both testaments of the Bible. Just as Elijah's mantle fell on Elisha when Elijah was suddenly taken to glory, so the Gospel torch will fall back into the hands of the Jewish people when the Church of true believers worldwide is suddenly removed. Therefore God's present work of the restoration of Israel should alert every born-again believer concerning the lateness of the hour.

But an untruth is being erroneously circulated in many churches, which undermines what the Bible calls our "Blessed Hope," the imminent appearing of our Lord and Savior in the clouds. The lie that's being taught is that the sudden appearance of the Lord to seize His Bride, the true Church, is a relatively new doctrine. The doctrine of the Pre-Tribulation Rapture is NOT new. It has always been in the Bible! If you ignore this truth, you may be tempted to watch for the Anti-Christ rather than the sudden appearing of the Lord Jesus!

In an effort to demean the doctrine of the Rapture, a smokescreen arose claiming that a Scottish girl in the 19th Century prophesied the doctrine and that it was popularized by Bible expositor James Nelson Darby. However, the apostle Paul wrote in 1st Thessalonians Chapter 4, "I wouldn't have you to be ignorant, brethren," .... ignorant about what? He said, "Don't be ignorant, ... we who are alive and remain shall be caught up together with the resurrected dead in the clouds, to meet the Lord in the air: and so we shall forever be with the Lord. "Therefore," Paul said, "comfort one another with these words." So the biblical doctrine of believers being caught up in the clouds at the sudden appearing of Jesus is supposed to be a comfort to every believer. Sadly, many preachers and websites deny the Pre-Tribulation Rapture and are sowing confusion in the Body of Messiah.

Many Bible teachers have written books about the Bible doctrine known as the Pre-Tribulation Rapture, but I believe this compilation of Bible scholarship by my friend Pastor Derek Walker is the best overall explanation of the subject. Pastor Derek writes with clarity and great conviction. The mysterious event known as the Rapture will be the turning point in the End Times, and the world will never be the same afterwards. When the restraining influence of the true believers is gone, the Anti-Christ will be able quickly to set up a global dictatorship and will require a mark on the right hand or forehead in order for people to buy or sell. If you miss the Rapture, beware of taking the mark of the beast!

I am very grateful for the many insights that I have gained from the books of Pastor Derek Walker over the years and am delighted that he is offering this book for the world, which must grasp this great Bible truth!

---

*Christine Darg is co-founder of the Jerusalem Channel and brings regular prophetic reports from the Holy Land. S he and her husband Peter have served the Lord for many years both with the Christian Broadcasting Network and Evangelist Reinhard Bonnke in Africa. Through JerusalemChannel.tv they bring Good News for the Last Days. Christine has authored a number of books including "Miracles Among Muslims" and "God Wants You Well." She regularly conducts prayer convocations in Israel.*

# *Introduction

This book is all about one of the most dramatic, momentous and glorious Divine Interventions of all time – the Rapture of the Church.   Our heavenly Bridegroom, the Lord Jesus Christ, will bring this Church Age to a close by personally returning to fetch His beloved Bride, before waging war on this godless world-system, which has rejected Him as its King, by pouring out His Judgments during the special time period called the Day of the Lord or the Tribulation.

This is the prophetic viewpoint known as the Pre-Tribulation Rapture, and it has become an issue of controversy, having attracted many critics.   In this book, I make the case for the Pre-Tribulation Rapture, answering the claims by its critics that it is just based upon inference, rather than clear statements of Scripture.  I show that if you strictly hold fast to a literal interpretation of Bible Prophecy, and are consistent in your use of the Biblical terminology, the Pre-Tribulation Rapture is indeed plainly stated by a number of passages of Scripture.  It is only by weakening the plain literal sense, and being fuzzy with terminology, that this truth is obscured.

But does it really matter?  Is not the timing of the Rapture just a theological question with little relevance to our lives?  Absolutely not!  This doctrine has great practical application to our Christian lives, and vision for the future, motivating us to give ourselves to that which has true eternal value.  It helps us to lift our eyes beyond the temporal things of this life to Christ above, and to our glorious eternal future with Him (Colossians 3:1-3).

The reason for the relevance and importance of the timing of the Rapture is found in the important New Testament doctrine of IMMINENCE, which says that the Lord's Coming for His Church is at hand, that He could return at any time. Jesus Himself declared that He will come, when we do not expect Him (Matthew 24:36,42,44), and then we will stand before Him at His Judgment Seat to give an account to Him for our works, to determine our eternal rewards for our faithfulness to Him (see Chapter 6).  If we really believed that Jesus could come at any time, even today, it would radically change our lives, powerfully calling us out of our complacency and compromise to live a higher life.  It gives us strong motivation to put Christ and His commands first, over our own man-made agendas, especially in living a life of holiness (obeying His Great Command to love Him with all our heart), and outreach through evangelism and discipleship (obeying His Great Commission). The importance of the imminence of the Lord's Return is confirmed by the strong and repeated emphasis placed upon it in the New Testament, which uses it as a major motivation for believers to live for Christ, so they are found ready at His imminent Return (see chapter 5).

The reason that it is important to uphold the Pre-Tribulation Rapture is that it is the only viewpoint that upholds imminence. If the Rapture was Mid-Tribulation, Post-Tribulation or near the end of the Tribulation (Pre-Wrath), then imminence is impossible, because many well-defined events (signs) would have to happen first, whereas imminence requires that nothing has to happen before the Rapture – for it is a sign-less event, that could happen at any time. Those who believe in the Bible but not the Pre-Tribulation Rapture know that many events have to take place before Christ Returns in His 2$^{nd}$ Coming. Therefore they have no expectancy that He might come for them at any time, even today. This results in a diminished zeal for Christ and a more casual attitude toward holiness, obedience and evangelism.

The Pre-Tribulation Rapture perfectly solves the major paradox of end-time Prophecy. On the one hand, Jesus described many clear Signs that must take place on earth before His Second Coming to earth in power and glory (Matthew 24:4-30 - this is confirmed by the Book of Revelation). On the other hand, Jesus also clearly said that His Coming would be imminent, as a thief in the night (Matthew 24:36-44). How can this be? The solution is clear – He first comes FOR His saints (to receive them to Himself), and then He returns WITH His saints to take possession of the earth. His Coming for His Church in the Rapture is imminent, but His 2nd Coming to earth is preceded by a sequence of Signs over a number of years.

In fact, all who take end-time Prophecy seriously (applying at least a degree of literal interpretation) agree that the Rapture of the Church (where Christ returns to the air, to call His Bride to Himself) is a distinct event to the 2$^{nd}$ Coming, when He actually sets His feet upon the earth to claim His possession of it. The difference between the views is simply in the relative TIMING of these two events. Those advocating the Pre-Tribulation Rapture point to a clear logical and Biblical reason for a time-gap of at least 7 years between Christ's Coming for His Church in the Rapture and His Coming to the earth in the 2nd Coming, namely that there is a period of time called the Day of the Lord or Tribulation, which is a time when God starts pouring out His Judgment (Wrath) upon the earth. These Judgments are initiated by Christ from Heaven, when He starts opening the Book with 7 Seals in Revelation 6. These manifestations of God's wrath will increase in intensity throughout the Day of the Lord before being brought to their climax at the 2nd Coming. This time of worldwide Judgment lasts at least 7 years, because it includes Daniel's 70th Week (Daniel 9:27). So the whole Tribulation is a time of Divine Wrath, and the New Testament plainly declares that the Church has been delivered and will be delivered from the Wrath of God (1Thessalonians 1:10, 5:9, Romans 5:9). Therefore, it makes perfect sense that Christ will remove His beloved Bride from the scene of Judgment, before He releases His Wrath upon the world.

What a wonderful revelation – that our heavenly Bridegroom is coming for us, to lift us up with Him into heavenly places, to be with Him forever, and that we should live in constant expectancy of this joyful union, motivating to prepare ourselves for Him by our holy devotion to Him and our obedience to Him in fulfilling the mission He denied for us in the Great Commission! So why has the doctrine of the Pre-Tribulation Rapture meet with such resistance and even mockery, by some in the Church? I would suggest a number of reasons:

Some see it as a doctrine of escapism, causing people to disengage from the world into a holy huddle waiting for the Rapture. But this is an entirely false representation of the Pre-Tribulation Rapture and its fruit. Although it does teach that God has provided us an escape from the coming time of Judgment (Luke 21:34-36, Revelation 3:10), this does not lead to escapism. On the contrary, knowing that we could suddenly meet with the Lord at any time, when He will judge our works, spurs us on to serve Him by reaching out to the lost with Gospel.

For others the idea that Christ could come suddenly at any time is an uncomfortable and disquieting thought, because they know their lives are not in order and they know they are not serving God as they should. Therefore the Pre-Tribulation Rapture disturbs their carnality, which is why they resist this idea. It is more comfortable to believe Christ's Coming is some way off yet, and so they still have plenty of time to get right with God. Believing that they will get much clearer Signs before His Return gets close, gives them the freedom to indulge their flesh a bit longer, before they finally repent and really put God first and serve Him fully.

For others, who are in the Kingdom Now (Dominion Theology) Camp, who have subjugated Christ's Great Commission to their own Dominion Mandate, to take over the kingdoms of this world and establish the Kingdom of God in His Name, the Pre-Tribulation Rapture is a doctrine that they hate, because it directly stands in opposition to their man-made project. The Pre-Tribulation Rapture causes us to focus our vision on the Lord in Heaven, so whatever we do on earth is the light of His imminent Return for us, which will propel into a glorious eternity with Him. Meanwhile Christ Himself will destroy the kingdoms of this world and establish His Kingdom on earth. This means our primary focus is evangelism and holiness, so we take as many people to Heaven with us as possible. Thus it focuses us on what Christ actually told us to do – gather a harvest of souls for Him in this Age by preaching the Gospel and making disciples (Matt 28:18-20, Mark 16:15-20).

However, for those caught up with a 'Kingdom Now' vision, the idea that Jesus could return at any time in the Rapture, and interrupt their kingdom-building totally disrupts and spoils their agenda to take over all the institutions of the world for Jesus. This clearly will take a significant time, and requires them to focus on our present life in this world, to increase our place and power in this world-system. For them, focusing on Christ's Return is a distraction for the job at hand, and so they need to discredit this Biblical teaching in order to establish their dominionist vision. In order to accommodate their vision (their uncommanded vanity project of taking over the world for God) for the future, they have to resort to non-literal interpretation of Prophecy - adopting the Post-Millennial view (the Church brings in the Millennial Kingdom, then Christ returns after the 1000 years of a Christianised world). But how do they explain away all the clear-cut end-time Prophecies of the Tribulation. One solution used is 'Preterism', which says all these prophecies were fulfilled in the destruction of Jerusalem in AD 70, leaving the way open now for the victorious Church to take over the world (see Appendix 2). But they forget that Jesus said that His Kingdom was not of or from this world, and would not be established by the efforts of His servants (John 18:36). He did not deny that He was a King (v37), or that His Kingdom would be established in this world, for He Himself will establish it from above at His Return (Daniel 2:34-45).

The Pre-Tribulation view is not against social action, but it affirms that the Great Commission is our primary purpose, and all our good works are secondary (they are not a substitute for the Great Commission). That is, everything we do, should have the ultimate Purpose of gathering a harvest of souls for the Lord. Remember Christ calls His Church (1) to Himself in HOLINESS by the Great Commandment to love Him with all our heart (Matthew 22:36-38), and (2) to embrace and join with Him in His mission of EVANGELISM to the world by the Great Commission (Mark 16:15-20, Matthew 28:18-20), shining our light in the darkness, which is the main way we love the lost (Matthew 22:38). Our real enduring legacy from this life and this Age that will abide throughout eternity is people, who we've brought to God and discipled (made into followers of Jesus).

So if you are comfortable in your life now and do not want to meet with Jesus any time soon, or if you want to build an earthly kingdom and legacy, you will not like the idea of a Pre-Tribulation Rapture. But do not reject this teaching on emotional grounds but check to see if it is Scriptural and change your vision and life accordingly.

Another false argument used against the Pre-Tribulation Rapture is that it denies the fact that the Church will go through tribulation (persecution), which it obviously does (John 16:33), and therefore when Christians face tribulation and suffer persecution they will get offended at God. This is based on a complete misunderstanding, related to the most popular name for 'the Day of the Lord', namely 'the Tribulation' (from Matthew 24:21,29). From this terminology they believe that 'the Tribulation' is simply an extension of the Church Age, which is generally characterised by tribulation, the only difference being it will be a time of increased persecution. However, although the Tribulation will indeed be a time of greatly increased persecution, especially through the rise of the antichrist, that is not the primary defining characteristic of this special period of time. Rather its key characteristic, which makes it completely different from the Church Age is that is a time of worldwide Divine Judgment and Wrath, from which there will be no escape for those on earth. This is reflected by its main proper title, used many times in Scripture: 'The Day of the Lord'. Therefore those who believe in the Pre-Tribulation Rapture do not do so out of fear of the wrath of antichrist (a common, misguided slur), but out of faith in Christ, who they know loves them and will deliver them from the coming Wrath of God.

To those who say faith in the Pre-Tribulation Rapture will render us unprepared for the antichrist, I would say that being martyred by the antichrist is not fundamentally different from being martyred by a totalitarian butcher of a more common variety. There is no special preparation given in Scripture except the revelation it gives about this final manifestation of evil, which is known to all Bible believers, whatever their particular viewpoint. Indeed, our preparation for all persecution is our unconditional faith in Christ and love for God, which is worked in our hearts through His Spirit and His Word. In fact, the teaching of the Pre-Tribulation Rapture focuses us on the Meeting that really matters, the Meeting that the Bible constantly emphasises, and that is not our meeting with the antichrist, but our Meeting with the Lord Jesus, when He comes for us in the Rapture, which will have eternal consequences for us (see Chapter 6). The denial of the Pre-Tribulation Rapture leads to the expectation that we will meet the antichrist before we will meet Christ, which causes people to primarily look for the antichrist, rather than looking for Christ, expecting His Return, and preparing to meet Him, which is the very thing that Scripture says that we should be constantly doing. Surely the Meeting we should be focusing on is the meeting with our Lord, not the antichrist. Therefore the Pre-Tribulation Rapture promotes a healthy, positive and biblical mindset of living hope in Christ, as we live in this dark and evil world.

In conclusion the Rapture will be one of the greatest and most dramatic and joyful events of all time, the climax of the Romance of Redemption, when Christ busting with love for His Bride, will demonstrate His love for her, by coming to deliver her from this evil world, and from the Wrath of God, so that she can be with Him and reign with Him forever as His eternal Bride-Wife. The Rapture will also be the catalyst for the Day of the Lord Judgments to begin, for Christ will be SEATED at God's right hand in the Church Age UNTIL it is time to subdue His enemies UNDER FOOT in the Day of the Lord (Psalm 110:1). Therefore the moment He leaves the Throne in order to return for His Bride in the Rapture, marks the time when the earth will move into a new period of time, the Day of the Lord, a time of Judgment. Immediately after the Rapture, we see the Church in Heaven (Revelation 4-5), and Christ (who is STANDING) opening the Scroll with 7 Seals, initiating the release of intensifying Judgments upon the earth (Revelation 6).

As well as the Rapture being an awesome Sign to the world that Judgment is about to suddenly fall as never before, it will also be manifestation of God's mercy to those who remain, for it will cause many who have been sitting on the fence to be saved. It is difficult to imagine the magnitude of the impact of the sudden disappearance of at least 1 billion souls from the planet, especially when all those who were raptured were Bible-believing Christians, and that this supernatural event was plainly predicted in the New Testament! Thus many will know that they now have a final chance to repent and trust in Christ for salvation before the judgments and horrors of the Tribulation overtake them. They will then know that the Bible is true, that Christ is truly the Son of God, who is faithful to powerfully save those who trust in Him as Lord (that will be clearly demonstrated by the Sign of the Rapture), and so many will get saved in the Tribulation as a result of the Rapture.

Studying Bible Prophecy (especially the Pre-Tribulation Rapture) gives us great hope and helps us understand the times in which we are living, and wakes us up, giving us a sense of urgency, so that we do not waste our lives, pursuing the wrong causes, because we have the wrong priorities. We are living in the last of the last days, the final generation of the Church Age. This means that the Coming of our Lord Jesus to receive us to Himself is very close, so that we need to make sure we are living holy lives before Him, and seizing every opportunity to serve Him and share the Gospel, for immediately after the Rapture, we will all stand before Him to give an account of our lives, and receive our eternal rewards.

# *Chapter 1 - The Teaching of Jesus on the Rapture

It was Jesus who initiated the New Testament teaching on the Mystery Church Age (Matthew 13), and He also gave the foundational teaching for the Rapture of the Church, that is part of this Mystery (1Corinth 15:51). The Rapture of the Church is the final event of the Church Age, the ingathering of the harvest of the Church, when Christ comes for His Bride (all believers in Christ, saved in the Church Age) and takes them to Heaven. The dead in Christ will be resurrected and we who are still alive will be raptured. The RAPTURE is the Coming of Christ for the Church in which He instantly 'catches up' all living believers to meet Him in the air and translates them into immortal bodies without experiencing death.

Jesus said in John 14:1-3: **"Let not your heart be troubled; you believe in God, believe also in Me. In My Father's House (HEAVEN) are many mansions; if it were not so, I would have told you. I go to prepare a place for you. And if I go and prepare a place for you, I will come again and receive you to Myself; that where I am, there you may be also."**

These are the words of a Bridegroom to His betrothed Bride, saying He will go away to Heaven, to prepare a home there for His Bride, where they will dwell together forever. He promises her that He will come again and receive her to Himself, to take her back to Heaven where their Marriage will take place. This foundational verse establishes a number of key truths about the Rapture, which distinguishes it from His Second Coming, when He returns in power and glory to take over the whole earth.

This is a Coming of Christ for believers only, unlike the 2nd Coming, which involves everyone. Its purpose is to be reunited with His Bride and take her to Heaven, whereas the purpose of the 2nd Coming is to judge His enemies and establish His Kingdom on earth. In John 14, Christ does not come and land on the earth and dwell (reign) here, as He does in the 2nd Coming (Zechariah 14:4), but He comes close to receive His Bride to Himself (in fact we will meet the Lord in the air - 1Thessalonians 4:15). He then returns with her to the place He has prepared in Heaven, where they abide during the period of Judgment on the earth, called the Day of the Lord, after which we will return with Him in His 2nd Coming (Revelation 19). Those who teach a Post-Tribulation Rapture, say that when Christ returns at the 2<sup>nd</sup> Coming, we will rise to meet Him in the Rapture, and then immediately do a U-turn and go back with Him to the earth. But this contradicts John 14, which says that when Jesus returns in the Rapture He takes us to Heaven.

Jesus also taught on the Rapture in His Olivet Discourse of Jesus (see my book: 'A Panorama of Prophecy' for a full exposition of the Olivet Discourse). This teaching of Christ was structured to answer the 3 Questions in Matthew 24:3:

*Question 1 asked for **the Signs of the Temple's Destruction** (in AD 70), which Jesus answered in Luke 21.

*Question 2 asked: **"What will be the Sign of Your Coming?"**, which He answered in Matthew 24:4-31, by describing the events in the Tribulation.

*Question 3 asked: **"What is the Sign of the End of the Age?"**
This is a different question than Question 2, but their answers are connected. The End of the Age is the Tribulation, so Question 3 is: "what are the Signs by which we can know when we are living in the time just before the Tribulation?" In other words, how do we know we are in the last days of the Church Age? Jesus answers this in Matthew 24:32-44 and Luke 21:28-36.

Notice that answering Question 3 after Question 2 requires Him to go back in time, from v31, which describes the final Regathering of Israel at the 2<sup>nd</sup> Coming, to v32ff which describes the time leading up to the start of the Tribulation. This is what interests us the most, being very relevant to us, for we are live in that time, the last days of the Church Age. In Part 1, we proved that Jesus' answer to Question 3 perfectly fits our unique times, confirming that we live in the last of the last days. Jesus answered Question 2 first because He needed to refer to His answer to Question 2 in order to answer Question 3. He expressed the connection between the answer to Question 2 (the conditions and events in the Tribulation), and Question 3 (the conditions and events in the time just before the Tribulation) in terms of TREES, because developing trees express the continuity of history. He uses TREES to describe all the different SIGNPOSTS in the world. For in the TRIBULATION, all the trees will come to their fullness, and are bear their fruit, as trees do in the SUMMER - either good trees bearing good fruit, like Israel (the FIG TREE), or evil trees bearing evil fruit. Other 'Tribulation Trees', like the Tree of advanced Technology, are neutral in nature. Once we know what the Tribulation Trees look like in the Summer, we can then know when we are in the SPRING time just before the Summer, because in the SPRING all these trees are budding, putting forth LEAVES in preparation for them bringing forth their fruit in the SUMMER.

Luke 21:28-32: **"Now when THESE THINGS** (that come to their fullness in the Tribulation) **BEGIN to happen** (in the time just beforehand), **look UP and lift UP your heads, because your Redemption** (in the Rapture) **draws near." Then He spoke to them a Parable: "Look at FIG TREE** (Israel – see Luke 13) **and ALL THE TREES. When they are already budding** (putting forth leaves in the SPRING) **you SEE and know for yourselves that SUMMER is now near. So you also, when you SEE THESE THINGS** (that will be in full manifestation in the Tribulation) **happening** (budding, beginning to happen), **know that the KINGDOM of God** (the Tribulation-Summer when the Kingdom starts to invade earth) **is near. Assuredly, I say to you, this generation** (who see these trees budding) **will by no means pass away till all things take place."**

So these SIGNS are like the initial appearing of TREES in the Springtime when they put forth their leaves, which is the sign that Summer is near, when they will be bearing all their fruit. Likewise, when we see them all these things begin to happen together, we know we are in the Spring time, just before the Summer heat of the Tribulation, when they will come to their fullness. That is why He used TREES to represent the SIGNS of the Tribulation, because trees, like world-conditions develop in a continuous way, and so they also tells us when we are close to the Tribulation. In my 'Panorama of Prophecy', I explain how this works for all the signs of the times, we are presently experiencing, proving Jesus is coming soon.

So Jesus compares the SIGNS to TREES, which are fully developed and bearing fruit in the Summer. When you see them all blossoming and putting forth leaves together in the Spring, you know that Summer is near. Likewise, since we know the various world conditions in the Tribulation (the Trees in their fully developed form), we can know when we are in the time just before the Tribulation, for they cannot become this way overnight. So when you see all these world conditions begin to develop together you know the world is getting close to the Tribulation. Now we can understand why God inspired Questions 2 and 3 to be asked together as a 2-fold Question: *"What will be the Sign of Your Coming, and of the End of the Age?"* It is because the answer to the 3rd Questions comes directly from the answer to the 2nd Question. Jesus said that when you see the Fig Tree

(Israel back in the Land) and ALL the Tribulation Trees spring up together then you know the Tribulation is near. In fact He went further and said that everything will be fulfilled within a man's lifetime from when these Trees start appearing.

## The Rapture of the Church

We've seen that after Jesus had answered Question 2 by giving the events of the Tribulation leading up to His 2nd Coming, He went back in time in order to answer Question 3 which asked for the Signs of the End of the Age (Tribulation). We will now study the last part of His answer, which gives the **Disappearance of believers in the Rapture of the Church** as the final SIGN that the world will see before the Judgment of the Tribulation falls upon the whole world.

In Luke 21:28 we saw He connected these Signs with the Rapture: **"When these THINGS** (SIGNS) **begin to happen, look UP and lift UP your heads, because your Redemption** (in the Rapture) **draws near."**

Many scriptures command the Church to wait, watch and look for the imminent Coming of Christ for us to take us to be with Him forever. Spiritually we are to be looking UP to Heaven where Christ is and from where He will suddenly return for us. He has not told us exactly when He will return, so we always have to stay ready. For us who see the signs of the approaching Tribulation we have all the more reason to look UP, for surely Jesus must be coming soon. Clearly the response Jesus wants from us who see these Signs is to adjust our spiritual focus, looking up to Jesus in heaven in expectation of the imminent redemption of our body in the Rapture, so our focus is on Jesus and our whole life is guided and motivated by the consciousness that any day we will rise to meet Him and stand before His Judgment Seat. This will motivate us to greater holiness, good works and evangelism.

The Church is restraining the final manifestation of evil. So the removal of the Church will result in a final sudden release of evil causing the Tribulation to begin. In the Tribulation, God allows evil to come to its fullness and judges it. Thus the Rapture is the final Sign to the world that the Tribulation is about to start. The Rapture is imminent, which means no one can know when it will happen - it's God's secret. Although the Signs we have seen so far give the general time, they do not reveal the exact timing of the Start of the Tribulation.

That is what Jesus says next in <u>Matthew 24:36</u>: **"BUT of that day and hour** (of the start of the Tribulation) **no one knows, not even the angels of Heaven, but My Father only."** Remember He is still answering <u>Question 3</u>, which asked about the timing of 'the End of the Age' or Tribulation. So God keeps the timing of the Rapture and Start of the Tribulation secret. He knows it, but does not reveal it to us, because we would probably misuse that knowledge. He wants to keep us on our toes, so that we always stay ready. He will come suddenly without warning, as a thief in the night. This is the Doctrine of Imminence - which is God's limitation on our knowledge of the time of the Rapture. He wants us to live as if Jesus could come anytime. So although we can't know the exact day of the Rapture, the general signs He gave us tell us that we are living very close to the end of the Church Age.

Then Jesus said in <u>Matthew 32:37</u>: **"For the Coming of the Son of Man will be just like the days of Noah."** Remember He is still answering Question 3 about the timing of the Start of the Tribulation, and having said no one can know its exact date, He now identifies it with the Coming of the Son of Man. This is saying that He will come to receive us in the Rapture before the Tribulation starts. In fact, the Rapture is the triggering event for the Start of the Tribulation. As we continue in His Prophecy, we will see that this truth is confirmed again and again.

Some assume 'the Coming of the Son of Man' here refers to the 2nd Coming, but that does not agree with the fact He is answering Question 3. Also the phrase: **"no one knows the day or hour"** always applies to the Rapture and NOT His 2nd Coming, because anyone in the Tribulation will be able to calculate the exact day of the Lord's Return. When Jesus said: **"the Coming of the Son of Man will be just like the days of Noah",** He was saying the events in the time of Noah in connection with the Flood are a TYPE or picture of what will happen in the time around His Coming in the Rapture and the Start of the Tribulation. The most obvious parallel is that **the Flood is the Type of the Tribulation,** for the Flood was the only previous worldwide judgment, and likewise the Tribulation is a worldwide judgment. Those who assume He is comparing His 2nd Coming with Noah's Flood forget the fact that the whole Tribulation is a time of worldwide Judgment, which has its climax at the 2nd Coming.

In <u>Matthew 24:37-39</u> Jesus compared His Coming to the days of Noah, making a 3-fold comparison, based on the 3 key phrases: 'BEFORE', 'the DAY', and 'the FLOOD'. Thus He is comparing (1) what happens before the main event, (2) what happens on the day of His Coming, and (3) the Judgment that falls immediately afterwards: **"The Coming of the Son of Man will be just like the days of Noah. For as in those days BEFORE the Flood they were eating and drinking, marrying and giving in marriage, until the DAY that Noah entered the Ark, and they did not understand until the FLOOD came and took them all away; so will the Coming of the Son of Man be."**

<u>The Parallels between the time of the Flood and the Tribulation.</u>

*1. He compared the general time BEFORE the Flood to the general time before His Coming.

*2. He compared what will happen ON THE SAME DAY as the Flood, immediately before it fell, to what will happen immediately before the Flood of Tribulation Judgement falls on the earth.

*3. He compared the FLOOD itself to the future judgment of the Tribulation, pointing out that it will be world-wide and therefore no one on earth will be able to escape its effects. He says that the result of both judgments is to take all the unbelievers away from the earth.

**\*1.** The time just before the Flood tells us what it will be like in the time just before the Tribulation. Jesus compared the Last Days of the Church Age to the time of Noah. The days before the Flood of Tribulation Judgments fall on the whole world will be like the days of Noah before the Flood of God's Judgment fell on the whole world. Thus the special characteristics of Noah's time will be repeated before the Tribulation. Jesus' characterised Noah's generation as just eating, drinking, marrying, giving in marriage. Now there's nothing wrong with these things in themselves, but there is no sign of any spirituality here. They were engrossed in their materialistic life and had no time for God. It indicates a society caught up in materialism and godlessness, forgetting God and pursuing purely natural things, and that certainly is a sign of modern life on earth. Also according to <u>Genesis 6</u>, great wickedness, corruption, lawlessness and violence covered the earth - a major public decline of all moral standards. <u>v1</u> also speaks of a population explosion in Noah's time. So we'd also expect a population explosion in the time leading up to the Tribulation, and this has certainly happened in an unprecedented way in the last 100 years. Man was advanced in knowledge before the Flood, evidenced by Noah's ability to build such a huge ship. The last 100 years have been marked by rapid scientific progress. So Jesus compared what will happen in the final days of the Church Age before His Coming and the start of the Tribulation to the time of Noah before the Flood.

Noah preached the Gospel to the world using His Ark as a visual aid. Likewise, in the closing period of the Church Age the Gospel will be preached to all nations, as Jesus said in Mark 13:10. The great explosion in world missions started in about 1800. There was a final period of 120 years of Grace during which Noah preached the Gospel, declaring that judgment was coming, but that God had provided a Way of Salvation, which was the Ark, a Type of Christ, so that all who trusted in God's Provision for would be saved from destruction. Those who were in the Ark were saved, being under its covering, for the Ark took the beating of the Flood instead of them. God told Noah to cover the wooden Ark with pitch, which was a red resin, in order to make it waterproof. So none of the waters reached those inside. Also the Hebrew word for pitch is also the word for covering or atonement. So the Ark covered with red pitch is a picture of Christ covered with His atoning blood, and all who take refuge in Him, come under the covering of His blood and are saved, because He took all the judgment we deserved. But those who reject Him will be swept away when judgment falls. But the people in Noah's day were so immersed in their godless, materialistic lives that they ignored all the warnings, and so were totally taken by surprise, when the Flood suddenly fell.

**Before the Flood, Jesus specifically described life in the world before the Flood as going on as normal, right up to the day of the Flood,** eating and drinking, marrying and giving in marriage (v38). The people had no idea that judgement was about to fall even though Noah warned them. Likewise, as in the Days of Noah, just before the Tribulation life will be carrying on normally, and they will even be saying: 'Peace and Safety.' **Therefore it follows that life on earth, even up to the Day the Lord comes in the Rapture, will also be going on as normal.** This is a clear contrast to events just before His 2nd Coming, for at that time it is at the end of the Tribulation, with God pouring out His Bowls of Wrath and the Battle of Armageddon raging and the sun turning to darkness. Life will be anything but normal! Thus the Flood is a type of the whole Tribulation and not just the 2nd Coming, for in the days just before the 2nd Coming, described in detail in the Book of Revelation, anything but normal life is going on. This is the Great Tribulation, the worst time ever, and Jesus said if He did not cut it short all flesh would be destroyed. This also proves the Coming of Christ in these verses is not the 2nd Coming, but the Rapture, which is a separate event before the Tribulation.

So Jesus emphasised that life just before the Flood was going on as normal, so they were all taken by surprise when the Flood suddenly fell. There were no special signs that it was about to fall. Likewise, the world will be taken by surprise when the Rapture happens and the Tribulation-Flood suddenly falls on them. There will be no special signs that the Rapture is about to happen. So the Rapture itself is a SIGNLESS EVENT, which can happen at any time, and it will happen suddenly, without warning, when you least expect it. Although Jesus gave Signs to give us a general idea when we are in the season just before the Tribulation, He emphasised that there would be no specific Sign, by which we could know the exact date of the rapture. Don't think that something dramatic must happen before the Rapture as a final warning, like a global crisis. In fact the world will be saying 'peace and safety.' There will be no announcement from heaven saying: '10 days to the Rapture!' Life will be going on as normal and then we will suddenly disappear. So there is a major difference in the Signs for the Rapture and the 2nd Coming. The Rapture is imminent, coming suddenly at an unknown time without any specific Signs. The 2nd Coming comes after a whole series of specific signs that will enable people to know the exact day.

In Matthew 24:37-39 Jesus pointed to 3 similarities between the days of His Coming and the days of Noah. First, the time before His Coming will be similar to the time before the Flood. Second, the Day of His Coming to initiate a period of judgment is compared to the actual Day that Noah entered the Ark. Third, world-wide judgement will suddenly fall on the world on the Day of the Lord's Coming, just as the world-wide judgment of the Flood suddenly fell on the very day Noah entered the Ark. Again this cannot be talking about the 2nd Coming, as this comes as the climax of 7 years of escalating world-wide judgements.

*2. Let us now consider the 2nd point of similarity - the Day of His Coming, which initiates the judgment. This is compared with the day that Noah entered the Ark, which initiated judgment. Initially this does not seem like an obvious similarity, until you realise that the final Sign to the world that the Flood was about to fall, the final event before the Flood, was the disappearance of all the believers into the Ark, when God removed them from the scene of judgement and lifted them above it, as Matthew 24:38-39 says, they were living their normal life: **"until the day that Noah entered the Ark, and did not know until the Flood came and took them all away, so also will the coming of the Son of Man be."**

Likewise, the final event before the Tribulation-Flood falls, the final Sign to the world that the Tribulation is about to start, will be the disappearance of the believers into Christ, when He comes for them in the Rapture. Just as God called Noah into the Ark, so Christ will return and gather His own to Himself in the Rapture. God will remove the true Church from the earth by lifting us above the scene of Judgment, before pouring out His Tribulation Judgments. Remember that He is still answering Question 3: 'What is the Sign of the End of the Age?' Having said there are no specific Signs for His Coming in the Rapture, He points out that there will be a final specific Sign to the world for the Start of the Tribulation - the disappearance of the believers in the Rapture. However, this is not a warning Sign, for the Tribulation will start immediately after the Rapture, so anyone who misses the Rapture will have to go into he Tribulation. Just as God shut the Door as soon as Noah entered the Ark, so He will shut the Door straight after the Rapture.

Then to confirm He is talking about the Rapture, Jesus gave a classic description of this Rapture of believers that happens in conjunction with His Return in Matthew 24:40-42: **"Then there will be 2 men in the field; one will be taken and one will be left. 2 women will be grinding at the mill; one will be taken and one will be left. Watch therefore, for you do not know what hour YOUR LORD is COMING."** He is talking about the parallel event to Noah entering the Ark and disappearing from view. Jesus will come and take the believers to Himself in the Rapture. The rest must enter the Tribulation. Notice He tells believers to be constantly on the alert for His Coming as they do not know when it will be. That's imminence. This repeats the early statement that no man knows the day, showing He is still talking about the same event. Notice when He says to believers to be Ready for: **"YOUR LORD is coming"**, the implication that He is coming for them, to take them to Himself. This verse does not describe His 2nd Coming when He comes to take unbelievers from the earth in judgment, but His Coming in the

Rapture when He comes to TAKE His believers to be with Him. This is confirmed in the next verses.

Some relate these verses to the 2nd Coming based on the fact that the word 'taken' also appears in the previous verse to describe unbelievers in Noah's time being 'taken' from the earth in judgment. However, this is a trick of translation. The 2 words translated as 'took' and 'taken' in these verses are actually 2 different words in the original Greek, so this argument backfires, for if Jesus wanted to make connect these 2 things He would have used the same word. When it says 'one was taken another left' the word for 'taken' is the same word that is used for when Joseph 'took' Mary to be with him as his wife (Matthew 1:24). So this is speaking of Jesus coming to take us to be with Him. This is the first hint that the Rapture is the Bridegroom coming to take His Bride.

Another argument people use is it can't be talking about the Rapture, as Jesus didn't talk about the Rapture, as it was part of the Mystery. That was left for the Apostle Paul to do. But this is a false assumption for we have seen that Jesus started to reveal the Mystery in Matthew 13, and it was given to Paul to complete it. Also we will see Jesus taught on the Rapture in John 14:1-3. Related to this is the assumption that the whole Olivet Discourse is about Israel and has nothing to say about the Church. This is a clumsy unjustified assumption, as the apostles represented both Israel and the Church, so the context should determine who is in view in any scripture. In fact, Jesus talks about Israel, the nations and the Church.

The final proof that Matthew 24:40-42 CANNOT refer to the 2nd Coming is that it contradicts the other scriptures of the 2nd Coming, especially the Judgment of the Sheep and Goat in Matthew 25. These tells us that at His 2nd Coming Jesus will gather all living Gentiles to Jerusalem to be judged, where they all stand before Jesus and are separated into those who are taken from the earth, and those who continue alive into the Kingdom. Thus the 'one taken another left' separation at the 2nd Coming takes place in one place, Jerusalem, whereas the 24:40-42 separation takes place throughout the world, wherever people are working or sleeping.

Then in Matthew 24:43-44, Jesus compared His Coming in the Rapture to a thief coming suddenly in the night to take the valuable things from the earth: **"But know this, that if the master of the house had known what hour the THIEF would COME, he would have watched and not allowed his house to be broken into. Therefore you also be ready, for the Son of Man is coming at an hour you**

**do not expect."** This is the first time that Jesus compares His COMING to a THIEF, who comes secretly and suddenly, unannounced, without warning signs, TAKING the things that are precious to Him, and then going away unseen. This is in total contrast to His 2nd Coming when He comes openly and visibly in manifest glory. The Rapture is a totally different kind of event to the 2nd Coming. Comparing His Coming with the coming of a thief seems shocking, but although He is taking the precious things from the earth (us), He is not actually a thief because He only takes those who belong to Him, who have given their hearts to Him. But to the world it will seem as if a thief has come when we all suddenly disappear. So it will appear to the world after the Rapture has happened, that a thief has come and taken multitudes of people. Now it is true that Jesus comes to take the precious things from the earth (His people), but of course He is not really a thief, for He will only take what belongs to Him. **To the world, He will seem to come as a thief, but for Us He will come as the Bridegroom for His Bride**, to rescue her from danger before waging war on the world-system under the power of the evil one.

The 'master of the house' who would try and stop Jesus coming to take His Church must be satan, the god of this world (2Cor 4:4), the ruler of this world (John 16:11), for the whole world lies in his power (1John 5:19, Eph 2:2). This reveals one of the differences between His Coming in the Rapture and His 2nd Coming, that absolutely requires them to be distinct events at different times. The 2nd Coming is signposted in such a precise way that anyone in the Tribulation (including satan) will be able to know exactly when Jesus will return (from Daniel and Revelation). In other words, this event is not imminent for us as it is at least 7 years away, and it won't be imminent for those in the Tribulation, for they will know when it is. This is one reason why satan gathers the world's armies to Israel just before Jesus is due to return there - in order to resist His arrival: **"the beast, the kings of the earth, and their armies, gathered together to make war against Him who sat on the horse and against His army"** (Revelation 19:19). So in the case of the 2nd Coming the master of the house does try and stop Jesus breaking into 'his house', for he knows when He will come. Needless to say, all his attempts to resist Christ are in vain! On the other hand, Christ's Coming as a Thief in v40-43 is imminent, for a thief doesn't announce when he will come. He keeps it a secret, so He might come at any time. Therefore the master of this world is not able to prepare any special resistance to Christ's Coming in the Rapture. Thus the very point Jesus is emphasising is the imminence of this phase of His Coming.

Therefore He concludes in Matthew 24:44: **"Therefore YOU** (believers) **also be ready, for the Son of Man is coming at an hour you do not expect."** So He is coming when you do not think He will. This is a strong statement of the imminence of His Coming in the Rapture. Whatever theory you may have as to why Jesus cannot come yet is contradicted by this verse. It is designed to humble us, by pointing out our lack of knowledge, because He has not revealed it to us. The Doctrine of Imminence says God has limited our knowledge in such a way that as far as we're concerned the Rapture could happen at any moment - so we always have to 'be ready.' Thus not only do we not know when He is coming (v36), we do not know when He is not coming (v44)!   Matthew 24:44 says that, not only does the world and satan not know, but believers also do not know, as Matthew 24:42 says: **"YOU** (believers) **do not know what hour YOUR Lord is coming."**

As a thief does not reveal when He is coming, so Jesus does not reveal the time of His Coming in the Rapture. His 2nd Coming on the other hand will have a clear 7-year Countdown, which Jesus outlined earlier in the Olivet Discourse. Therefore the Coming of the Lord in these verses is a distinct event from His public 2nd Coming.   Actually I prefer to say that the 2nd Coming is in 2 Phases.
**In the first Phase He comes FOR His Church in the Rapture, then 7 years later in the 2nd Phase, He will come WITH His Church in power and glory.**
In the 1st Phase the Lord comes to initiate the Day of the Lord, the worldwide judgment of the Tribulation. In the 2nd phase the Lord comes on the Great and Awesome Day of the Lord, the climactic day of the Day of the Lord, to conclude and complete this worldwide judgment, and establish His Kingdom on earth.

Notice Jesus made repeated statements of Imminence since Matthew 24:36, confirming that He has been talking about the same event throughout - His Coming as a Thief to take the believers to Himself. **"But of that day and hour no one knows"** (v36), **"Watch therefore, for you do not know what hour your Lord is coming"** (v42), **"Therefore you also be ready, for the Son of Man is coming at an hour YOU do not expect"** (v44). Also this demonstrates this is the main feature of this phase of His Coming that He felt it was important to emphasise. Now previously in the same talk in Matthew 24:7-30, He described in great detail all the SIGNS leading up to the 2nd Coming, giving the 7-year Countdown according to Daniel's 70th Week. But now in <u>Matthew 24:36-44</u> He emphasises that His Coming is an imminent and therefore SIGNLESS event. There's only 1 solution to this paradox: His Coming is in 2 phases. He comes 1st as a thief, and 2nd in manifest glory.

We have seen that in v37-39, Jesus pointed to 3 similarities between the days of His Coming and the days of Noah: (1) just as in the days of Noah normal life went on until the day the waters of the Flood started to fall, so normal life will be going on right up to the day the Tribulation Judgments start to fall. It will happen suddenly with no special warning signs. (2) Just as the key event that marked the transition to sudden Judgment in the days of Noah was the disappearance of the believers into the Ark, so the key event that marks the transition into the Tribulation is the disappearance of the believers into Christ when He comes in the Rapture. So the final thing that will happen before the Tribulation Judgments fall will be the removal of the believers into Christ - the Ark of our Salvation.

**\*3. What happens immediately after.** Just as Noah's Flood started to fall on the same day he entered the Ark, so the Tribulation Flood will start to fall on the same day as His Coming in the Rapture. In both cases it is a worldwide Judgment, so no one on earth will be able to escape it. Thus worldwide Judgment will suddenly fall on the world on the day of His Coming, just as the worldwide Judgment of the Flood suddenly fell on the very day Noah entered the Ark.

<u>1Thessalonians 5:2</u> agrees with this when it says: **"the Day of the Lord** (Tribulation) **will come just like a THIEF in the night** (the Rapture). **While they are saying, "Peace and safety!" then destruction will come upon them suddenly like labour pains on a woman with child, and they will not escape."** The fact that the Tribulation starts on the same day as the Rapture means that His Coming to remove the believers in the Rapture is what initiates the time of Tribulation Judgement. We can understand why there is this connection in 2 ways.

(1) 2Thessalonians 2 says the Church, indwelt by the Holy Spirit, is presently restraining the spirit of antichrist, but when the Restrainer is removed in the Rapture the forces of evil are released to come into full manifestation especially through the antichrist, and this is one of the special characteristics of the Tribulation.

(2) Another characteristic of the Tribulation is that it is a time of Divine Judgment and Wrath upon the whole world, like Noah's Flood. But God has promised the Church that He has delivered us from the Wrath of God, so it would not be righteous of God to subject the Church to the Tribulation Wrath of God. Therefore God must remove His believers to a place of safety before releasing His Judgment. Since this Judgment is upon the whole earth, He must first come and remove us from the earth, and then there is no more reason to delay His Judgment, so immediately after the Rapture He begins the time of Judgment. Therefore, it will be just as in the days of Noah. First, God separated and removed the believers, so that they were lifted above the waters of the Flood, above the scene of Judgment. Then, as soon as He had made the believers safe, He immediately released His Judgments on the earth. Likewise Jesus will return and lift us above the earth, removing us from the scene of Judgment, and then He will immediately start releasing the judgments of the Tribulation.

Jesus confirmed this in a similar passage in Luke 17 where He compared this time to the days of Lot. v28 says: **"It will be the same as happened in the days of Lot: they were eating, they were drinking, they were buying, they were selling, they were planting, they were building."** The days leading up to the Tribulation Judgement are likened to the days leading up to the judgment of Sodom and Gomorrah. From one point of view it is life as normal with no obvious sign that the judgment is about to fall. In fact these towns were very prosperous. But from another point of view we know there was great immorality that was not only accepted, but also publicly approved and promoted by the society.

Then Jesus said in Luke 17:29-30: **"but on the day that Lot went out from Sodom it rained fire and brimstone from heaven and destroyed them all. It will be just the same on the day that the Son of Man is revealed."** Again we see that God removed the believers from the scene of the Judgment, before releasing His Judgment on the cities. Clearly as in the days of Noah, God withheld His Judgment until He had removed the believers, for He would not be just in pouring out His wrath on the righteous. Now we can understand why the very same day the believers were removed, God's Judgment fell from Heaven. Jesus said that the same thing would happen when He comes to save us and reveal Himself to us in the rapture. First, He will remove us from the scene of Judgment, which is the earth, and then on the very same day He will initiate the Judgments of the

Tribulation. It is significant from the story in Genesis 18 that Christ Himself came to earth with His angels to rescue Lot and to initiate the Judgment of the cities. He will do the same at the Tribulation. Since the time of Divine Judgment starts at the beginning of the Tribulation, not at its end, all these passages speak of a Coming of the Lord before the Tribulation, to save His own and initiate Judgment, as well as His Coming at the end of the Tribulation.

Matthew concludes this section of the Olivet Discourse with a Parable, which emphasises the importance of taking the doctrine of imminence seriously.

Matthew 24:45-51: **"Who then is a faithful and wise servant, whom his master made ruler over his household, to give them food in due season? Blessed is that servant whom his master, when he comes, will find so doing. Assuredly, I say to you that he will make him ruler over all his goods. But if that evil servant says in his heart: 'My master is delaying his coming' and begins to beat his fellow servants, and to eat and drink with the drunkards, the master of that servant will come on a day when he is not looking for him and at an hour that he is not aware of, and will cut him in 2 and appoint him his portion with the hypocrites. There shall be weeping and gnashing of teeth."**

This demonstrates the positive influence of believing in imminence on our behaviour. The good servant knew his master could come at any time, so was determined that his master will find him doing good when he comes, and so he maintained a constant faithfulness and so received a good reward at His Coming. The evil servant rejected imminence and assumed his master would DELAY his coming, so was not looking for his master. Without the consciousness of the master's imminent arrival, he felt free to behave badly and mistreat those under him, until the master took him by surprise. In this case his evil behaviour demonstrated an unregenerate spirit, although he called himself a Christian and had a position in the church. He was a hypocrite in that he professed outwardly to follow Christ, but that was not what was in his heart. So when the master returned he consigned him to a place of punishment with the rest of the unbelievers. Likewise, when Jesus returns He will consign all unbelievers (including 'Christian' ones to the wrath of the Tribulation on earth, and if they still do not repent, they will end up under everlasting wrath in hell.

We complete our study of the Olivet Discourse, with the concluding words of Jesus in the parallel passage in Luke 21, which emphasise that the Tribulation will be a worldwide judgment from which there will be no escape for those who are on the earth, just like the Flood in the days of Noah.

After describing the events of the Tribulation, Jesus said in Luke 21:34-36: **"Take heed to yourselves, lest that Day** (the Day of the Lord or Tribulation) **come upon you unawares. For it** (the Tribulation) **will come as a snare** (a trap that will suddenly snap tight) **shall it come on ALL those who dwell on the face of the whole earth** (it will be a world-wide Judgment). **Watch therefore and pray always, that you may be COUNTED WORTHY to ESCAPE** (through the Rapture) **ALL these THINGS** that **shall come to pass** (in the Tribulation)**, and STAND** (in a transformed body) **before the Son of Man."**

Jesus promises to provide an escape from the Tribulation-Trap, for those 'counted worthy.' They will escape from 'all these things' of the Tribulation that will come on all those who are on the earth. He doesn't talk about enduring through these things. This escape is the Rapture. Instead of going through the Tribulation, we will stand in our new bodies before the Son of Man, and give an account before the Judgment Seat of Christ. Since the events of the Tribulation come upon all those on the earth, the only way to escape all these things is to be removed from the earth, and this is exactly what Jesus will do in the Rapture to those counted worthy (righteous) through their faith in Christ. They will be lifted up from the earth and find themselves standing before the Son of Man in their glorified bodies. The only way to escape ALL these things is by a Pre-Tribulation Rapture, for a Mid-Tribulation or Postulation Rapture would only be an escape from SOME of these things. Now since the Tribulation is world-wide and affects ALL who dwell on the earth, and since these 'worthy' ones are promised an escape from 'ALL these things' that will take place on the earth, it is obvious that this escape must involve a removal from the scene of judgement, which is the whole earth, BEFORE 'all these things' of the Tribulation take place.

Thus the teaching of Jesus is that before the worldwide Judgment of the Day of the Lord falls, He will return as a thief to take the believers to Himself. So as far as the world is concerned, the initial act of Judgment of the Day of Lord is when Jesus gets up from sitting at the right hand of the Father and returns to receive His own to Himself. By removing the Church He is removing His restraint upon evil, allowing it to come to fullness in order for it to be judged. This action also allows Him to move in greater Judgment. Thus the Day of the Lord begins with the Coming of the Lord to rapture His Church and then continues to the end of the Tribulation as He continues to pour out His Judgments.

This agrees with the 2 examples Jesus used for this event:

(1) God removed Noah into the Ark before the Flood fell, raising him above the earth and the waters of judgment, rather than protecting him underwater.

(2) God removed Lot from Sodom, the scene of Judgement, before sending the Judgement down, rather than preserving him through the bombardment. There is no language here of preservation through Judgement.

Jesus confirms this in Revelation 3:10 where He does not just promise believers protection from Judgment, but deliverance from the very time-period of the Tribulation Judgment: **"I will keep you from the hour of trial which shall come upon the whole world, to test** (all) **those who dwell on the earth."** Therefore to fulfil this promise God must provide an escape FROM THE EARTH ITSELF for those counted worthy before the Tribulation begins. This exactly describes the Pre-Tribulation Rapture! Then He adds that once they have been removed from the earth their new location will be standing in the very Presence of Christ in their resurrection bodies.

Therefore Jesus will come to take His chosen ones to Himself, gathering them together to Himself just before 'all these things', that is all the events of the Tribulation come to pass on the earth. Thus Luke 21:34-36 is a plain statement of the Pre-Tribulation Rapture! Notice that these verses describing the removal or taking of true believers into the Presence of Christ before the Tribulation, confirms that when He talked earlier about one being taken and the other left behind, it was referring to the taking of believers in the Rapture, and not the taking of unbelievers in judgment at the 2nd Coming.

So, how one can be 'counted worthy' to be in the Rapture? This language agrees perfectly with the Gospel. No sinful man could actually be worthy of receiving salvation or anything from God. But it does not say they are worthy, but they are 'counted worthy' and there is only one way anyone can be 'counted worthy' of salvation or 'reckoned as righteous' before God, and that is through receiving the imputed righteousness of Christ as a free-gift. On the Cross Jesus accomplished the Great Exchange in Himself of our sin for His righteousness, so that when we receive Christ our sin was imputed to Him and His righteousness was imputed to us as a totally free-gift of His grace. Only in this way are we counted worthy of Salvation. The Rapture is part of our Salvation by Grace. It's not a reward for good works, because the judgment of our works for rewards happens after the Rapture at the Judgment Seat of Christ. Our spirit was saved when we were born again, our soul is now being saved by God's Word, and our body will be saved at the Rapture, thus completing our Salvation by Grace. So this isn't talking about a partial rapture where only the best Christians will make it but the rest must go through the Tribulation. This is unbiblical. We are not made worthy through our own efforts. We can only be counted worthy by accepting Christ and being clothed in His righteousness. All truly born again believers will be raptured and stand before Christ on that day. If you have prayed and accepted Christ then you will be counted worthy, because you have turned from trusting in yourself and your works, and put all your trust in Christ and His work for you.

### *So how can you be RAPTURE READY?
**(1) Receive Jesus as your Lord and Saviour.**
**(2) Prove the genuineness of your faith by a changed life.**

If Jesus is truly your Lord and Saviour, you are in Christ, and you will go up in the Rapture. What will happen immediately after that is that you will stand before His Judgment Seat and receive your eternal reward based on your faithfulness to Him in this life, and this could happen at any time! Let the imminence of the Lord's Coming inspire you to a consistent holy life, so that you are ready to meet Him when He returns.

1John 3:1-3: **"Behold what manner of love the Father has bestowed on us, that we should be called children of God!... Beloved, now we are children of God; and it has not yet been revealed what we shall be, but we know that when He is revealed, we shall be like Him, for we shall see Him as He is. And everyone who has this hope in Him purifies himself, just as He is pure."**

## *Chapter 2: The Romance of Redemption

It was Jesus who initially taught on the Rapture in the Olivet Discourse. We have seen that to the world His Coming in the Rapture will be like a THIEF in the NIGHT. Jesus also taught in John 14 that for the Church it will be like the BRIDEGROOM coming for His BRIDE to take us home and be with Him forever.

John 14 records His tender words as the Bridegroom promising His Bride, that although He must go away and prepare their marital home, He will come again to fetch her to be with Him. John 14:1-3: **"Let not your heart be troubled; you believe in God, believe also in Me. In My Father's house are many mansions; if it were not so, I would have told you. I go to prepare a place for you. And if I go and prepare a place for you, I will come again and receive you to Myself; that where I am, there you may be also."** This will be fulfilled in the RAPTURE. This is our blessed hope the glorious appearing of Jesus Christ for His Bride. He is coming soon to take us home. Redemption is a Divine Romance, which comes to a climax in the Rapture.

In those days, the Bride did not know exactly when the Bridegroom would return for her, so she had to prepare herself and always stay ready. Right now the Church needs to be preparing for that romantic moment when her Bridegroom comes and rescues her from the time of Tribulation, lifting her up into His Presence. The Tribulation is a time when Christ wages war on the world-system. What Bridegroom would leave His beloved bride in a place that He was about to bombard, if He had the power to extract her? Surely He will rescue her from this terrible time of God's outpoured Wrath!

Knowing the marriage customs of Bible times gives much insight into Bible Prophecy and the Romance of Redemption (God's ultimate purpose in saving us).

*1. The marriage is planned and arranged by the father of the Bridegroom, who chooses a bride for his son. Likewise the Father planned a marriage for His Son and chose the Church as his Bride.

*2. The Father negotiates with her family and a Bride Price is paid, representing her value. The price paid for the Bride was the Blood of Jesus. He came the first time to win His Bride by demonstrating His love, laying His life down for her and thus paying the Bride Price.

*3. Once the agreement was made, they would eat and drink wine together, signifying they were now in covenant. At this point the couple are BETROTHED. Likewise when we receive Christ, accepting His offer to belong to Him, we are BETROTHED to Him. Paul said in 2Corinthians 11:2: **"I betrothed you to one husband, so that to Christ I might present you (to Him) as a pure virgin."** We now belong to Christ, united to Him by covenant through His Blood, destined to become His wife.

*4. Gifts would be given to the Bride from the Bridegroom.
Likewise, gifts and blessings are poured upon us by Christ through the Holy Spirit.

*5. They may never have seen each other face to face.
We have not seen Jesus face to face, but we love Him and eagerly await His return.

*6. After the Betrothal the Bridegroom goes away to his Father's house promising to return. There he prepares the marital home. Only when the father says everything is ready can the son return. Likewise, Jesus has gone to Heaven to prepare a place for us and has promised to come back for us.

*7. Meanwhile the Bride makes herself ready to presented to Her Bridegroom in the beauty of holiness, her beauty not merely external, but that which comes from a devoted heart. She prepares her wedding dress to be dressed like a Queen. She wants him to be pleased when he looks upon her. She keeps herself pure, for all her hopes are now looking toward the day of her marriage when she will see her Bridegroom face to face and be with him forever. Likewise, we prepare ourselves for when we will see Him face to face as 1John 3:2-3 says: **"we know that when He is revealed, we shall be like Him, for we shall see Him as He is. And everyone who has this hope in Him purifies himself, just as He is pure."** We are sanctified by the Blood and the washing of the Word, so that when He returns we will be ready. Our wedding garment will be His glory corresponding to our good works, which He'll release in us at His Return when He rewards us according to our works.

*8. No one knows the exact time of the Wedding, which happens when the Bridegroom returns for His Bride. Even she does not know exactly when he'll come for her. She must stay ready even if he seems delayed. Likewise no one knows the time of Christ's Return for His Bride in the Rapture. He tells us: "I'm coming quickly." There's great excitement in heaven & earth as the time gets near.

*9. At the father's signal, when he judges all things to be ready, the bridegroom returns for His bride. Likewise when the Bride is ready and complete, when the full number are saved, then the Father will turn to the Son and says: "Go, get her, Son!"

*10. The Bridegroom dressed as a King goes in joyful procession with his friends to the Bride's house. There is great excitement. He enters the house and carries the Bride out, and brings her back to the place he has prepared for her.

Likewise, when Jesus returns for His Church it will be to TAKE His Bride home to be with Him forever. In the Rapture of the Church He comes in a joyful procession with shouts and trumpets and we will be lifted up to meet the Lord in the air. This is a romantic moment as He carries off His Bride, delivering her from the Tribulation, in order to be with Him forever.

*11. Back at his house, she makes her final preparations to be ready for brief family Wedding Ceremony, including putting on her wedding dress.

Likewise, back in Heaven, the Bride is prepared to be presented spotless and glorious to Christ. To be ready, she must go through the Judgment Seat of Christ first, where she is cleansed from all unworthy, dead works that she is wearing. She is also rewarded for her good works with a corresponding glory that will be released through her and that will radiate out of her, which is now her clothing.

*12. In the Wedding Ceremony the bride is unveiled and presented to the bridegroom in all her beauty and they see each other face to face, for until now she has been veiled. They are now MARRIED and she is His WIFE.

Ephesians 5:25-27: **"Christ loved the Church and gave Himself for her that He might sanctify and cleanse her with the washing of water by the word, that He might present her to Himself a glorious Church, not having spot** (no physical blemish) **or wrinkle** (no sign of age) **or any such thing** (no imperfection), **but that she should be holy and without blemish** (inwardly pure and perfect)."
Likewise, at this point Christ and His Church will be MARRIED, and the BRIDE will now become the WIFE of the Lamb and they will reign together forever as King and Queen. We will have our eternal marital home in the New Jerusalem.

In a vision of the Church in Heaven just before the 2nd Coming this Wedding Ceremony has already taken place. Revelation 19:7-8: **"Let us be glad and rejoice and give Him glory, for the Marriage of the Lamb has come** (happened)**, and His WIFE has made herself ready. And to her it was granted to be arrayed in fine linen, clean and bright, for the fine linen is the righteous acts of the saints."** Now having passed through the Judgment Seat of Christ where her dead works were consumed by fire, she is now dressed only in white glorious linen, shining with the Glory of God according to the reward she received for her good works that received approval at the Judgment Seat.

*13. The couple next go into a special bridal-chamber where the marriage is consummated. Likewise, the Church has 7 years in heaven before the Marriage Feast, of close 'face to face' fellowship with Christ where our union with Him will be brought to completion on every level, His glory filling our whole beings.

*14. They then appear together and lead a procession to the Marriage Feast. The herald cries: **"the Bridegroom comes!"** so that the invited guests know to come to the Feast. Christ will return to the earth with His Church, as HUSBAND and WIFE, in His 2nd Coming, for the Marriage Feast, which takes place on earth. In Revelation 19:7-8, we saw the WIFE in heaven dressed in white linen.

Then v9-14: **"Blessed are those who are called to the Marriage Supper of the Lamb!' ... Now I saw Heaven opened, and behold, a white horse. And He who sat on him was called Faithful and True** (the HUSBAND)**, and in righteousness He judges and makes war. His eyes were like a flame of fire, and on His head were many crowns...and His Name is called The Word of God. And the armies in heaven, <u>clothed in fine linen, white and clean</u> followed Him on white horses** (this is the WIFE according to the previous verses)**."**

This confirms that the Rapture must take place before the 2nd Coming.

*15. The invited guests join in the celebrations, which will last a week at the start of the Millennium. General invitations had already been sent out to friends to invite them to the Wedding so they could be ready to come. When it was time, they are bidden to come to the Feast. Among the Wedding-Guests for this Feast will be the believers on earth at the end of the Tribulation. During the Tribulation, the Gospel of the Kingdom will be preached inviting all people to be come and be part of this Feast and the Kingdom. But only those who are ready, who have received

Christ and have OIL in the LAMPS (that is, the Holy Spirit in their spirits), only these will be able to enter into the Feast and the Millennium. The unbelievers with no oil will be excluded. This is the scenario of the Parable of the 10 Virgins in Matthew 25, when Jesus returns with His Wife to earth at the end of the Tribulation for the Marriage-Feast. These virgins are not the Bride but the companions of the Bride in the Feast. They are the people alive on the earth when the Bridegroom returns with His Bride. When He comes He separates these ones into 2 groups depending on whether they are ready or not.

So the Rapture (7 years before) is part of a joyful wedding procession with shouts and trumpets as the Bridegroom comes to TAKE His Bride to Himself to be with Him forever face to face, fulfilling His love for her. He delivers His Bride from this evil world and lifts her up to a higher life with Him. In the time in between the betrothal and the wedding, the Bride must prepare to meet Him and be ready for when her Bridegroom comes for her.

**Pictures of this 'Romance of Redemption' are seen in Old-Testament Marriages, which are Types of Christ and the Church. Ruth** is redeemed by **Boaz** and becomes his wife, and **Esther** who after a long period of preparation and beautification is presented before the King who then marries her. Other Marriages also contain pictures of the Rapture. For example:

**\*1. ADAM and EVE** (Genesis 2:18-25). God had a Plan for us before sin came in, which was revealed before the Fall in the Marriage of Adam and Eve - a picture of Christ and the Church. His Plan is more than saving us from sin. It's for us to be eternally united with Christ as His Bride. Adam is a type of Christ. God's purpose revealed in Adam is fulfilled in Christ. It is not God's best for Christ to rule alone. So Genesis 2:21-22 says: **"The Lord God caused a deep sleep to fall on Adam, and he slept; and He took one of his ribs, and closed up the flesh in its place. Then the rib which the Lord God had taken from man He made into a woman, and He brought** (presented) **her to the man."** He received her as His wife saying she was: **"bone of my bone and flesh of my flesh"** (v23). Likewise, the Father provided a Bride for Jesus through His sleep of death. This 'sleep' represents an aspect of Christ's death that has nothing to do with sin. Rather, it is the laying down and giving up of His life to release it to us and to make His Bride. In death, His side was opened and out came blood and water. The Church was taken out of Christ being brought forth from His side. The Church was created from Christ's own life and spiritual DNA and so corresponds to Him and qualifies to be His Bride. Eve was formed out of a wound in Adam's side. She derived her life and nature from Adam. She was built and prepared by God to be presented to and meet her future Husband. She was perfect like him and became one with him, sharing his dominion. In all these ways, Eve is a picture of the glorious Church. At the Rapture the Church will be presented before Christ in perfection and with the same words of acceptance, Christ will own her as His Wife forever.

**\*2. ISAAC and REBEKAH** (in Genesis 24) is another story of a marriage made in heaven - a picture of the Divine Romance. Isaac, the only beloved son of Abraham, who had previously been offered as a sacrifice in Genesis 22 is a type of Christ. They both experienced a death and resurrection after which they both received their bride. The Chief Servant (Eliazer, which means Helper) is a Type of the Holy Spirit and sent by the Father, to find a Bride for His son. Rebekah, the chosen Bride, is a type of the Church. Likewise, the Father sent the Spirit to the earth to find and call out a Bride. As the Gospel is preached He calls her to come to Jesus and receive Him as her Head. Meanwhile Isaac remained in his inheritance. Likewise, Jesus remains in Heaven while the Bride is being called and prepared. Finally, the Bride will be brought to the Bridegroom.

Rebekah responded positively to the Servant, who glorified Isaac, telling her all about him, his sacrifice, his character, his rich inheritance, and the promises and covenant from God that assured his future. She would be able to partake of all of these things in Isaac. This is a picture of the Spirit preaching the Gospel to every person, calling them to Christ. Then he proposed to her and called for a decision. If it was a 'no', he would go elsewhere. Rebekah believed him and said 'yes.' When we say 'yes' to Jesus, we are then betrothed to him, even though we've never seen him. Abraham had told the Servant to TAKE a wife for Isaac, which was only accomplished when she stood before Isaac. First, He called her. Then, He led her on a journey to Isaac leaving her old-life behind. Finally, she was presented to Isaac to be his wife. Likewise, the Spirit first calls us to Christ. Then, He takes us out of our old-life in the world and takes us on a new journey with Him that has a heavenly destination where we will stand before Jesus. Finally, at the Rapture we are taken into Christ's Presence to be His Wife.

The decision was Rebekah's. In v57 she was asked: **"Will you go with this man?"** And she said: **"I will go."** She decided to leave the old-life and start at once on the new journey with the Servant This journey is a picture of the present Christian life in this world. She was now following the leading of the Servant, who knew the way. Now Isaac was the most important One for her. Likewise, we are called to leave the old-life and walk in the Spirit, Who leads us closer to Jesus. On the journey she didn't see Isaac, but believed in him and was committed to him, rejoicing in the hope of seeing him. It was a long difficult journey of faith to reach her final destination and permanent inheritance. But she had a Personal Guide and Helper. On the journey the Servant told her all she wanted to know about Isaac and his inheritance. In the hardship she was inspired by the thought that the journey was temporary and soon she would be with her Isaac forever. Her thoughts were focused on when she would see him. The last time Isaac was seen was when he was sacrificed. The next time He is seen is when He comes to meet his Bride. He has been waiting for her and preparing a place for her. As Rebekah reached the end of her journey, Isaac came for her out of his dwelling place.

Likewise at the end of the 2000-year journey of the Church, Jesus will come out from heaven for His Bride. At the Rapture, Jesus will come down from heaven and signal the Spirit to take us up to meet Him in the air, just as Rebekah was taken up to meet Isaac. Then Rebekah saw Isaac for the first time, and he took Rebekah and she became his wife and he loved her. This speaks of the consummation of our salvation at the Rapture, when we will enjoy eternal face-to-face fellowship united with Him and sharing His glory, authority and inheritance as His beloved Wife. As Rebekah was brought into Isaac's presence, to dwell with him as his wife, so in the Rapture, we will be lifted up, transformed and presented before Christ as His glorious Bride. This is when the Marriage takes place, and we will be eternally united with Him as His wife.

### The Song of Solomon

**\*3. A 3rd picture of the Divine Romance and my personal favourite is the SONG of SOLOMON,** which gives a wonderful picture of the love relationship between Christ and the Church. It is the story of Solomon, who is a type of Christ. His beloved, Shulamith, is a type of the Church. Shulamith is the feminine form of Solomon, and both names mean peace. One day King Solomon, dressed as a Shepherd and not as a King, goes to the countryside and inspects his flocks. In his travelling, he comes across a young country girl who is looking after her family's vineyards and they fell in love. He initially presented Himself to her as a Shepherd lover because He wanted their relationship to be based on love, rather than on force, with her being overwhelmed by His kingly power. This is a picture of Christ's 1st Coming, clothed in a human nature, dressed as an ordinary man, with His majesty veiled. He didn't come as the King in all its glory, for then we would be forced to submit to Him because of His power. Rather He wanted a relationship with us based on love. He came dressed as the Good Shepherd wanting to win our heart with His love, not His power. He wants us to love Him for Who He is in Himself. The couple enjoy a wonderful courtship where He revealed Himself as a loving Shepherd. He declared his love for her and awoke her love under the apple tree. Likewise Christ demonstrated and declared His love for us under the Tree of Calvary.

Once they had got to know each other, at some point He would have had to give her an amazing revelation about Himself, saying: "There's something I have to tell you. I am not just a shepherd, I am also the King." She would have laughed, but as she looked at him again, she'd have realised he was serious. She had to trust him and accept it by faith without seeing His Majesty, and she did believe Him. Likewise, when Jesus tells us: "I am not just the Good Shepherd, I'm also the King of kings", we know He is true and we believe Him even though we have not seen His glory. Then Solomon proposed, she accepted and they became betrothed, declaring vows of undying love to each other. Then he said he had to go away up to Jerusalem to prepare a place for her in the royal palace and get everything ready for the wedding. But he also promised that when all was done He will return and take her to be with him as his wife. This is the promise Jesus gave us in John 14. Until she sees him again she has to trust his word and prepare herself for the great day when he returns for her, and not be discouraged by the ridicule of unbelievers. Likewise we must believe the Lord's promise to come back for us, and prepare ourselves for the day of the Rapture. You can imagine what happened when she told her family the young man she had been seeing was actually King Solomon, and that one day he will return and take her to Jerusalem! They really thought she was in a fantasy world, and so they put her out to work hard in the vineyards. Likewise the world thinks we are crazy, when we say my Jesus is coming again as King of kings.

But one day Solomon returns in power and glory as described in chapter 3. This time, he is not dressed as a Shepherd, but as the King in all His glory with all his mighty men with him. Likewise Christ will return for us at the Rapture with His angelic guard of honour. The whole town asks: **"Who is this coming with such a great procession."** As it gets closer, they say: **"It is King Solomon on the day of his wedding with all his mighty men."** Then the procession turns in their little town, and as Shulamith looks, she recognises the King as her Shepherd-Lover. He has come for her! He gets out and walks to her house and lifts her up and takes her away back to Jerusalem where they are married and have a Wedding Feast. This is a wonderful picture of the Rapture of the Church, after which the unbelievers realise that she was telling the truth all the time.

The Song opens at the wedding feast with her now as the Queen, sitting at table with Solomon and the ladies of the court. She tells them her story, explaining why her skin is so tanned as her brothers had put her out to work hard in the vineyards. She tells them all about Solomon, and the story of their courtship up to that point and also their developing relationship including their first night together. It is the most beautiful picture in the Bible of the Divine Romance, which is why it is called the Song of Songs, just like the Holy of Holies.

# *Chapter 3:  Paul's Teaching on the Rapture

Having seen that Jesus taught the Pre-Tribulation Rapture, that is, the Rapture will happen just before the Tribulation starts. We will now go on to Paul's teaching on the Rapture. First of all, Paul taught that the Rapture is part of the Mystery in 1Corinthians 15:51-53: **"Behold, I tell you a MYSTERY, we will not all sleep, but we will all be changed, in a moment, in the twinkling of an eye, at the last trumpet; for the trumpet will sound, and the dead will be raised imperishable, and we will be changed. For this perishable** (body) **must put on the imperishable, and this mortal** (body) **must put on immortality."**

This is logical because the whole Church-Age was a MYSTERY hidden in God in the Old Testament times and only revealed by Christ and the apostles. This Age ends with the RAPTURE of the Church from the earth. So the Rapture is part of the Mystery. This means the Rapture of the Church was not revealed in the Old Testament, and therefore Jesus was the first one to reveal it. Now the resurrection of the righteous dead when the Messiah comes to establish His Kingdom at the end of the Tribulation is not a Mystery, for this was clearly prophesied in the Old Testament, but what is new is the Rapture of the Living, their mortal bodies being changed to immortality. Since the Rapture is a Mystery it must be a distinct event from the resurrection of the dead at Christ's 2nd Coming. To explain this let us first of all define the Rapture:

*DEFINITION: **The RAPTURE is the Coming of Christ for the Church in which He instantly 'catches up' all living believers to meet Him in the air and translates them into immortal bodies without experiencing death.**

Not only was this transformation of living believers not prophesied in the Old Testament, but it seems to contradict the Old Testament prophecies of the Messianic Kingdom, for if all believers are raptured at the Lord's Return, there would be no one left to populate the Messianic Kingdom, for all unbelievers are killed at Christ's Return. The only solution to this paradox is that the 2nd Coming of Christ is in 2 phases. First He comes for His Church, to take us to be with Him in the Rapture, then after a period of time (actually 7 years) He will return in power to repossess the earth. During this time many will be saved and those who endure to the end of this time will inherit the Messianic Kingdom.

## 1Corinthians 15

1Corinthians 15:51-52 describes what will happen to us in the Rapture: **"Behold, I tell you a Mystery; we shall not all sleep, but we shall all be changed, in a moment, in the twinkling of an eye, at the last trumpet; for the trumpet will sound, and the dead will be raised incorruptible, and we will be changed."** 'Sleep' refers to the state of a Christian's body when it has died, because God will wake it up again on the resurrection morning. The event that Paul describes here applies to those believers who are alive at Christ's Coming in the Rapture. Paul himself had a strong hope of being in the Rapture for he says: **"WE will be changed."** He was not wrong in this, but had this hope because he correctly believed in imminence, that the Rapture could happen at anytime. This doctrine of immanency is also seen here when it says we will be changed 'in a moment'. This is the word 'atomos', which means an atomic second, the shortest possible moment of time. He also said it will happen in the twinkling of an eye, in the time it takes for a photon of light to reflect off your eye. In other words it will happen suddenly, with no warning. We will suddenly find ourselves standing before the Lord. Many times Jesus says: 'I am coming soon', but this is a poor translation. It really means: "I am coming suddenly or quickly"-again a statement of imminence. For us living in the end times we can also say 'Jesus is coming soon', because of all of the Signs of the Times that are fulfilled.

Then Paul describes the amazing change that will take place in our bodies in v53-57: **"For this corruptible** (body) **must put on incorruption, and this mortal** (body) **must put on immortality. So when this corruptible has put on incorruption, and this mortal has put on immortality, then shall be brought to pass the saying that is written: "Death is swallowed up in victory." O Death, where is your sting? O Hades, where is your victory?" ... thanks be to God, who gives us the victory** (over death) **through our Lord Jesus Christ."**

Finally in v58 he applies this truth to our life: **"Therefore** (in view of the Rapture), **my beloved brethren, be steadfast, immovable, always abounding in the work of the Lord, knowing that your toil is not in vain in the Lord."**

The teaching on the Rapture is very practical. It will motivate you to be steadfast when things get hard, helping you fix your eyes on the prize at the end of your race. When it says your toil or labour in the Lord is not in vain, this is referring to the fact that when you are raptured you will stand before the Judgment Seat of Christ for rewards. The Rapture is the completion of our salvation when our bodies are saved from the presence and power of sin, and transformed into immortal bodies, just like that of Jesus Christ.

ICorinthians 15:20: **"Now Christ has been raised from the dead, the first fruits of those who are asleep."** The first fruits of a harvest represented the whole harvest. The offering up of the first fruits to God was the guarantee of the rest of the harvest. In other words, Jesus' Resurrection body is the prototype for our resurrection bodies.

1Corinthians 15:50: **"flesh and blood cannot inherit the Kingdom of God."** Therefore our new bodies will not have blood. Instead our body will be filled with the Glory of God. The glory of God in our spirits will be fully released in and through our bodies.

Philippians 3:20-21: **"Our citizenship is in heaven, from which we also eagerly wait for the Saviour, the Lord Jesus Christ who will transform our lowly body that it may be conformed to His glorious body, according to the working by which He is able even to subdue all things to Himself."** Our bodies will be changed to be just like Jesus' resurrected glorified body! As the HEAD, so the BODY, for we are completely united to the HEAD forever.

Ephesians 5:27 says that after the Rapture we will be presented: **"a glorious church, not having spot or wrinkle or any such thing** (all marks of the Fall removed), **holy and without blemish."** Jude 24 says God is able to: **"present you faultless before the presence of His glory with exceeding joy."**

*Paul's letters to the Thessalonians are full of teaching on the Rapture.

1Thessalonians 1:10: **"We are to wait for His Son from Heaven** (not the antichrist from hell), **whom He raised from the dead, even Jesus, who delivers us from the wrath to come."** We are to wait for Jesus who will come for us. When He comes He 'delivers us from the wrath to come.' His delivering us from Wrath is directly connected to His Coming. Now Jesus has already delivered us from the Wrath of Hell by His Blood. So this Wrath to come must be a different Wrath. It must be the wrath of the Tribulation. So Jesus must come before the

Tribulation in order to deliver us from the Wrath of the Tribulation. So Jesus will come to deliver us from the Tribulation! We are not told to look for or expect the Tribulation and the antichrist, but to wait with expectancy for Christ to come and save us from it, by means of the Rapture, for we have been delivered from all judgement, wrath and condemnation. God has promised the Church deliverance from all of God's wrath, for Jesus has taken it all upon Himself. This includes the deliverance from the Tribulation, since it is a Time of Divine Wrath.

### 1Thessalonians 4

Later in 1Thessalonians 4 Paul describes how the Lord will do this. The classic passage on the Rapture is 1Thessalonians 4:13-18: **"But we do not want you to be uninformed, brethren, about those who are asleep, so that you will not grieve as do the rest who have no hope."** It seems that they understood about the Rapture of the living, and expected it to happen anytime. But they did not know what would happen to believers who die before the Rapture. They were concerned that some of their departed brethren would miss out on this wonderful event.

v14: **"For if we believe that Jesus died and rose again, even so God will bring with Him those who have fallen asleep in Jesus."**

Paul encourages them that the dead in Christ will be resurrected at the same time. Although their bodies are in the grave, their spirits are in Heaven, and when Jesus returns He will bring their spirits with Him, and they will be reunited with their bodies and receive resurrection bodies.

v15: **"For this we say to you by** (according to) **the Word** (teaching) **of the Lord** (in other words Paul's teaching on the Rapture agrees with and expands the teaching of the Lord), **that we who are alive and remain until the Coming of the Lord, will not precede those who have fallen asleep."** He talks about 2 groups of believers, (1) those who are alive and (2) those who are sleeping at the Lord's Coming. He calls the 1st group: **"we who are alive"**, again showing that Paul believed in imminence and himself lived in the expectancy that he would be alive for the Rapture. Considering the Signs of the Times we have all the more reason to believe that we will be part of the rapture generation who will never die.

<u>v16</u>: **"For the Lord HIMSELF will descend from Heaven with a shout, with the voice of the archangel and with the Trumpet of God, and the dead in Christ will rise first."** 'HIMSELF' emphasises the personal nature of the Rapture. This is not something He can delegate for this is the Bridegroom coming to fetch His Bride. Notice the magnitude of this event - it is the Trumpet of God, not of an angel or man. Those who put the Rapture at Mid-Tribulation tend to identify the Rapture Trumpet with the 7th Trumpet of Revelation. But the 7th Trumpet is an angelic trumpet releasing judgment, whereas the Rapture Trumpet is the Trumpet of God calling a great assembly of believers to meet Christ in the air. He tells them there is no need to be concerned for those who have died in Christ, for they are not going to miss out. In fact they are going up first! Notice there is no partial rapture here. Those who go up are: 'the dead in Christ.' The only requirement is that they are in Christ. Being in the Rapture is part of our salvation by grace independent of our work. Therefore the only requirement for the living to go up is that they are in Christ. It will not be a dismembered Bride that will be presented to Christ.

<u>v17</u>: **"Then we who are alive and remain will be CAUGHT UP together with them in the clouds to meet the Lord in the air, and so we shall always be with the Lord."** We get the word 'rapture' from this verse. The word 'rapture' is from the Latin verb 'rapto' which was used to translate of the Greek word 'harpazo' translated as 'caught up'. It means 'to seize or snatch away' suddenly. We will all suddenly be caught up and find ourselves rising and meeting the Lord in the air. It will be a huge meeting in the air of the whole church whether dead or alive. No earthly stadium is big enough so God has use the atmosphere!

The Coming of the Lord and the 'catching up' to meet Him will be like a MAGNET coming down over a box of different materials. Only those with the same iron-nature as the magnet will go up. Things that look like they are made of iron, but are really plastic, will not go up. Thus plastic, pretend Christians will not go up. But anyone who is born-again, with Christ within them, will be drawn up to meet Christ in the clouds by a powerful attraction! When it says: **"so we shall always be with the Lord"** this reveals the purpose of the Rapture - the Divine Romance, the Bridegroom coming for His Bride to be with each other forever.

v18: **"Therefore comfort one another with these words."** The teaching of the Pre-Tribulation Rapture is a comfort. But if it is after the Tribulation, then they would not be concerned for those who fell asleep. In fact, they would be happy for them, as they will not have to go through the Tribulation.

### 1Thessalonians 5

In 1Thessalonians 4:15-18 the apostle Paul described the Rapture claiming that his teaching on this was according to the Lord's own teaching (v15). Then he continues on the same theme in 1Thessalonians 5 by addressing the issue of the timing of the Rapture and the Tribulation, using the same language and coming to the same conclusion as the Lord in His teaching.

v1,2: **"But concerning the times and the seasons** (the timing of the Rapture and the Tribulation) **brethren, you have no need that I should write to you** (for he had already taught them on this). **For you** (believers) **yourselves know perfectly that the Day of the Lord** (that is, the Tribulation)**, so comes** (starts) **as a THIEF in the night."** In agreement with the teaching of Jesus, Paul is saying here that the Day of the Lord will start suddenly, without warning, with the Lord's Coming as a Thief to take His own in the Rapture, according to the very language used by Jesus. 'The Day of the Lord' here is the Tribulation, for the whole Tribulation is a time when the Lord intervenes directly in Judgement.

This is confirmed by v3: which gives more detail about the start of the Day of the Lord, confirming that it refers to the Tribulation, not to the 2nd Coming of Christ: **"For when they** (the unbelieving world) **say: "Peace and safety!" then sudden destruction** (the Judgment of the Tribulation) **comes upon THEM** (on the world, not the church)**, as LABOUR PAINS upon a pregnant woman, and they shall not escape."** He describes the time just before the Day of the Lord as being apparently normal, where people are even saying: 'Peace and safety.' Then He describes the start of the Day of the Lord judgments as the sudden onset of labour pains, which then continue intensify until the Birth (the 2nd Coming). Thus the Day of the Lord is the time of labour pains, a classic definition of the Tribulation.

This is very the language Jesus used to describe the start of the Tribulation, comparing it with the sudden onset of Labour Pains (Matthew 24:8), from which there will be no escape, signifying that this is a worldwide Judgment that takes place over a period of time. So when v2 says 'the Day of the Lord' starts as a thief in the night, Paul is talking about the start of the Tribulation, and saying that it is initiated by the coming of a thief, which is the very language used by Jesus to describe His Coming in the Rapture. The Bible is consistent in its use of language. Paul knew the teaching of Jesus and was expounding it. So when Paul referred to the coming of a thief, he was speaking of the Rapture. So v2 says the Day of the Lord or Tribulation starts with the Coming of the Lord in the Rapture as a thief in the night. So this is a plain statement that the Tribulation begins suddenly with the Rapture, and it will be a total surprise to the world. This confirms the teaching of Jesus that the Tribulation will start immediately after the Rapture. This means that when the Thief comes He must remove something that had been preventing the Judgement, so that when it is removed the result is a sudden onset of destruction. This is speaking of the Church, which Jesus will remove from the earth when He comes. This also explains why there is a clear distinction between 'you' (believers) and 'them' (unbelievers) in this passage, for these 2 groups will experience the Rapture and Tribulation in 2 very different ways.

Notice that it is the unbelieving world, not the Church that experiences the Rapture as a thief in the night and the Tribulation as Birth Pains that start suddenly. 1Thessalonians 5:2-4: **"The Day of the Lord** (the Tribulation) **so comes as a THIEF in the Night. For when THEY say: 'Peace and safety', then sudden destruction comes upon THEM** (not on us)**, as LABOUR PAINS upon a pregnant woman. And THEY** (the unbelieving world) **shall not escape** (the Day of the Lord, unlike the Church, which will escape in the Rapture)**." But YOU, brethren** (believers have a different destiny)**, are not in darkness, so that this DAY** (the Day of the Lord or Tribulation) **should overtake YOU as a THIEF."** He clearly distinguishes the experience of believers (referred to as YOU) and unbelievers (referred to as THEY) in relation to the Day of the Lord. He says specifically that the sudden destruction of the Tribulation will come on THEM, but not on YOU (the Church). Notice how he contrasts the experience of believers and unbelievers. Having said unbelievers will experience His Coming as a thief, as they discover multitudes of people have suddenly been taken away from the earth, Paul affirms here that the believers will NOT experience His Coming as a Thief.

So the Day of the Lord will overtake unbelievers like a Thief, again confirming that the Tribulation is initiated by the Coming of the Lord as a Thief to take His own in the Rapture. The world will experience the Rapture as if a Thief has come, after a billion or more people are suddenly taken from the earth. On the other hand, the Church-Age believers will NOT experience the Rapture as the coming of a Thief, but as an escape from the darkness of the Tribulation, being rescued by our Bridegroom. So we will not have to face this time of Judgment. On the other hand the world will not escape the Day of the Lord Judgment, for it will suddenly come upon and overcome them. This will not be the experience of the Church because it will be raptured. So it is the Lord who initiates the time of worldwide Judgement called the Day of the Lord, by coming as a Thief to remove the Spirit-filled Church from the earth, and in so doing He will remove the restraining force on the antichrist and evil generally. This results in the birth pains of the Tribulation starting suddenly with great destruction all around the world, and intensifying until the Return of Christ.

Having said that the unbelievers will not escape the Labour Pains of the Tribulation, Paul affirms that the Tribulation will not overtake the believers (as a thief). He gives the reason for this difference. Unbelievers are in DARKNESS, that is, they are in the kingdom of darkness, which God starts to judge in the Tribulation. But believers are in the LIGHT, not the darkness, and so they do not come under the Judgment of the Tribulation. So our experience of the Lord's Coming will be different from the world. For the world He is an unknown Thief who surprises them and removes the valuables from the earth, but for us, He is our Bridegroom coming for His Bride to take us home to Heaven.

He goes on to reaffirm that as sons of the light, we are not part of the kingdom of darkness, but the kingdom of light, so we do not belong to the darkness of the Tribulation, when the kingdom of darkness is being judged by the kingdom of light. Instead we belong in the Light of God's Glory. v5: **"You are all sons of**

**light and sons of the day. We are not of the night nor of** (the kingdom of) **darkness."** So we must make sure we are alert and ready for the Lord's Coming.

<u>v6-8</u>: **"Therefore, let us not sleep, as others do, but let us watch and be sober. For those who sleep, sleep at night, and those who get drunk are drunk at night. But let us who are of the day be sober, putting on the breastplate of faith and love, and as a helmet the HOPE of SALVATION."**

Hope relates to the future. So the hope of salvation is talking about our expectation of a future salvation, the salvation of our body, which takes place at the Rapture. So the salvation he is talking about here is not the salvation of our spirit, but of our body in the Rapture. We are to put on this hope as a helmet. A helmet covers our mind and directs our vision. These prophetic truths are a necessary part of our spiritual armour, protecting our mind. Whatever battles we face, we must have our helmet firmly fixed on our head, especially the vision of the imminent Coming of the Lord to save us in the Rapture.

Paul again talks about this future salvation when he concludes in <u>verse 9</u>: **"For God did not appoint us to Wrath** (to the Tribulation)**, but** (instead) **to obtain Salvation** (in the Rapture) **through our Lord Jesus Christ."** We are not appointed to wrath, but instead to obtain Salvation from this Wrath. So, we are not appointed to go through the Tribulation, but to receive Salvation from the Tribulation-Wrath, when Jesus returns for us in the Rapture. At that time we will also receive the Salvation of our bodies.

<u>v10</u> confirms that this Salvation through Jesus is not something that has already happened, but something that will happen when Jesus comes for us in the Rapture: **"who died for us, that whether we wake or sleep** (whether we are alive or dead at the Rapture)**, we should live together with Him."** This reflects the language of 1Thessalonians 4 that all believers, dead or alive, will receive a release of resurrection life in their bodies at the Rapture, and taken to be with Him forever. So instead of experiencing the wrath of the Tribulation, Jesus will return and save us in the Rapture, transforming our bodies and delivering us from this wrath by removing us from the earth.

Another confirmation that Paul has continued to talk about the Rapture in 1Thessalonians 5 is in <u>verse 11</u>: **"Therefore comfort each other and edify one**

**another just as you also are doing."** This is very similar to what he said at the end of his classic description of the Rapture in 1Thessalonians 4. Again we see that the Teaching of the imminent Pre-Tribulation Rapture is a great comfort and encouragement for believers inspiring us to be found ready when He comes.

### The Thief in the Night

We conclude with a final look at the expression that Paul used to describe the Coming of the Lord in the Rapture: 'the thief in the night.' This term originates with Jesus who compared His Coming with sudden, unexpected coming of a thief. He said in <u>Luke 12:39,40</u>: **"If the master of the house had known what hour the THIEF would come, he would have watched... Therefore you also be ready, for the Son of Man is coming at an hour you do not expect."**

**To the WORLD, THE RAPTURE will be the coming of a THIEF in the night, taking the precious things from the earth. But to the CHURCH the Rapture is the coming of the BRIDEGROOM for His BRIDE.**

<u>Other verses also talk about the thief in the night</u>.

<u>2Peter 3:10</u>: **"the Day of the Lord will come like a THIEF."**

<u>In Revelation 3:3 Jesus says</u>: **"I will come like a THIEF, and you will not know at what hour I will come to you."**

<u>Revelation 16:15</u>: **"Behold, I am coming like a THIEF. Blessed is the one who stays awake."**

**<u>What the comparison of the Rapture with the coming of a Thief tells us</u>:**
**\*1. The RAPTURE is IMMINENT**, which means it can happen at any time. A thief does not tell the house what time he is coming, neither does he give them any kind of warning sign. Likewise the Rapture will be unannounced. There will be no special warning signs for it. Life will be going on as normal on the earth. Some say the Church must be glorious first, so it cannot happen for a long time, but the glorification of the Church can only be fulfilled after the Rapture. Whatever theory you may have why Jesus can't come yet, remember that He warned us that He would come at a time when we do not expect Him.

<u>Luke 12:40</u>: **"be ready, for the Son of Man is coming at an hour you do not expect."** So not only do we not know the time of the rapture, for Jesus said 'no man knows the day', but we also don't know any time when it can't take place, for

He said He will come at a time when we do n0t expect Him. He is saying that we cannot know, because He has not revealed it to us, so we can only speculate. So He deliberately keeps us in suspense, for He could come at any time.

Likewise Matthew 24:40 says: **"Be on the alert, for you do not know which day your Lord is coming."** He is talking to believers here, so it's not just the world that does not know the day. Then in v42 He said: **"be ready; for the Son of Man is coming at an hour when you do not think He will."**

**\*2. Like a thief in the night, Jesus will come when the world is in darkness and asleep. The Rapture will be unexpected.** The world will be taken off guard and unprepared. The Rapture will happen suddenly and take the world by surprise, but those who are awake will are ready for Him

**\*3. Jesus comes like a thief to take the precious jewels (the believers) from the house (the earth).** To the world, it will look like a thief has come, taking people from the earth. But He's not really a thief because He only takes what belongs to Him. We belong to Him, because He has purchased us with His blood. He is coming to claim His own - to snatch us away from the earth and take us back to His home in Heaven. The word used for the Church being 'caught up' is the same as that used for Philip's sudden translation in Acts 8 and Paul's 'catching up' to heaven in 2Corinthians 12

**\*4. The thief comes suddenly**, takes what he wants and then leaves quickly. When Jesus says 3 times at the end of the Bible in Revelation 22: **"I am coming soon,"** this really means: **"I am coming quickly."** Remember we saw that the whole event will be over in a moment, in the twinkling of an eye. He will come, do His work and go unseen and the world and the world asleep in the darkness won't see Him or be aware of Him. All they will be aware of is that something valuable has been taken from them. Although 1Thessalonians 4 describes the Rapture as a noisy event, it will probably only be noisy in the Spirit, so only believers will hear the trumpet in their spirit calling them to rise to meet Jesus. As far as the world is concerned it will happen secretly, as if a thief had come. (It is possible that all will hear a short loud noise but not understand it).

**On the other hand, His 2nd Coming will be totally different kind of event.** When He comes at the end of the Tribulation it won't be as a thief. He will come publicly manifesting His power and glory, so that every eye will see Him. The 2 descriptions of His Coming, as a Thief and as the King of kings, are so opposite to each other, they could not be more different. Therefore they must be descriptions of 2 different phases of His Coming.

## 2Thessalonians 2

In our study of Paul's teaching on the Rapture, we now go to 2Thessalonians 2, which confirms that in the Tribulation, after the Church is removed, evil is allowed to come to its fullness through the antichrist, and God responds by increasingly pouring out His wrath on the world system.

2:1: **"Now brethren, concerning the Coming of our Lord Jesus Christ and our Gathering together to Him."** Clearly the Rapture is the subject under discussion. This is important to bear in mind in interpreting the next verses.

v2: **"that you not be quickly shaken from your composure or be disturbed either by a spirit** (a false prophecy) **or a message** (a false teaching), **or a letter as if from us, to the effect that the Day of the Lord** (the Tribulation) **has come."** Some were teaching that the Day of the Lord, the Tribulation, the time of antichrist's dominion, had already come. Again it is clear that the Day of the Lord here cannot refer to the 2nd Coming, for they surely knew Christ hadn't yet returned in power and glory. Rather, they were troubled by the teaching that they were in the Tribulation, no doubt thinking one of the Emperors like Nero was the antichrist. This would have been all the more troubling if they had been taught by Paul that they would be raptured before the Tribulation.

Remember that in 1Thessalonians 5, Paul had clearly defined 'the Day of the Lord' as the Tribulation, and it makes no sense that he changed the meaning of this expression in his 2nd letter. Many assume that 'the Day of the Lord' here refers to Christ's 2nd Coming in glory, but that makes no sense, because the idea that the 2nd Coming had already happened would have been silly. Jesus taught that when He returns the whole earth will see Him in His glory. Paul's disciples were well taught and would not have been disturbed by such reports. Some translations try and make sense of this by translating it as: "that the Day of the Lord is at hand", that is, it is about to happen, but this violates the normal meaning of the Greek used here. Also 'the Day of the Lord' here cannot mean 'the Rapture', for they were not troubled that the Rapture had come, because it had obviously not come. Neither were they troubled that the Rapture was about to come, for they would be happy about that, not troubled. The only meaning that makes sense and is consistent with other scriptures is that the Day of the Lord is the Tribulation. They were being troubled by people saying that the Tribulation had started. Some even used Paul's name in vain saying he'd written a letter to that effect. Naturally, they were troubled by this, for Paul had taught them that the Rapture will be before the Tribulation. But now this hope was disturbed by this report that they were now in the Tribulation, without being delivered from it by the Rapture as they had expected.

In the next verses, Paul puts them right by affirming the Pre-Tribulation Rapture. First of all he told them not to believe this false message in v3: **"Let no one in any way deceive you, for that Day** (the Day of the Lord, the Tribulation) **will not come until the APOSTASY** (or DEPARTURE) **comes first, and** (then) **the man of lawlessness** (the antichrist) **is revealed, the son of destruction."**

Much confusion has arisen around the word translated 'apostasy', which affects the whole meaning of this verse. Other translations have it as 'falling away.' It is the Greek word 'apostasia.' Its basic meaning is simply: 'Departure.' (Since the translation of 'apostasia' is so central to the correct interpretation of this passage, I have devoted Appendix 1 to this important issue). In fact, the oldest English translations translated it as 'Departure'. Now, in 1Timothy 4, Paul does talk about 'departure' or 'falling away' from the faith in the last days, referring to apostasy. Perhaps the translators assumed he was talking about the same thing here, and so translated it 'apostasy'. But this is an unjustified assumption. It does not say that the Departure in v3 is a Departure from the Faith. It does not explain what the departure is, but simply calls it THE Departure. Paul is talking about a specific Departure, but does not directly tell us what this Departure is and what it is from. Therefore, he thinks it should be obvious to the readers, as if we should know which Departure he is talking about. He cannot have assumed that they knew it was 'the Departure from the Faith' that he had described to Timothy, as 1Timothy had not even been written yet. Since he does not explain it in the verse, it must be clear from the context. Since he does not specify what this Departure is, rules of Bible interpretation dictate that we should look in the context of previous verses to see what Departure that Paul is talking about, and it is right there in v1, where he introduces the subject under discussion: **"concerning the Coming of our Lord Jesus Christ and our GATHERING together to Him."**

So let us translate the verse in a way that helps us to keep an open mind on this issue: **"for that Day will not come unless THE DEPARTURE comes first."** If we look in the context, it becomes obvious what this Departure is. Not only is there a Departure there, but Paul had even underlined the fact that it was the main subject under discussion! That's in v1 where he says: **"Now brethren, with regard to the Coming of our Lord Jesus Christ and our GATHERING together to Him."** What Departure is he talking about? Clearly it is the DEPARTURE of the Church from the earth in the RAPTURE. So we can translate v3 as follows: **"Let no one in any way deceive you; for the Tribulation will not come unless the RAPTURE comes first, unless the Departure of the Church happens first."** It is a plain statement of the Pre-Tribulation Rapture. The whole passage now makes sense. He is confronting the false teaching that they were in the Tribulation, by saying that was impossible, because the Tribulation cannot start until the Departure of the Church. Clearly the presence of the Church on earth prevents the Tribulation from happening, and Paul explains why this is the case in the next few verses.

So he is talking about the Rapture, the Departure of the Church from the earth. In v3 Paul is saying that the Tribulation will not start until the Rapture comes first, and then immediately after that the antichrist will be revealed, who is destined for destruction. We know from other scriptures that the start of the Tribulation is marked by the rise of antichrist on the world-stage. In Daniel 9:27 he is revealed at the start of the 7 years when He makes a covenant with Israel. When the 1st Seal is opened in Revelation 6, he is the Rider on the white horse going forth to conquer. So the Tribulation starts with the antichrist being revealed.

So the antichrist will only be revealed after the Rapture, and it also says this in v3: **"Let no one in any way deceive you, for that Day** (the Tribulation) **will not come until the DEPARTURE comes first, and** (then) **the man of lawlessness is revealed, the son of destruction."** They were worried that the Tribulation had started, which means they would have to face the antichrist. Paul's answer was that the Tribulation will only start and the antichrist will only be revealed after the departure of the Church, so they won't be there for the Tribulation or antichrist. Thus the Rapture happens first followed by the Tribulation when antichrist will be revealed. So the Tribulation can't begin and antichrist can't be revealed until the Church departs from the earth in the Rapture. So they have no grounds for concern.

In verse 4 Paul describes what antichrist will do when he becomes world-ruler at Mid-Tribulation: **"who opposes and exalts himself above every so-called**

**god or object of worship, so that he takes his seat in the Temple of God, displaying himself as being God."**

Then he explains why the antichrist cannot be revealed until the Church is removed. It is because the Holy Spirit through the Church is a powerful restraining force against the spirit of antichrist in <u>v6-8</u>: **"and now you know WHAT restrains him** (antichrist) **now that in his time he will be revealed. For the mystery of lawlessness is already at work; only HE who now restrains will do so until He is taken out of the way. Then that lawless one will be revealed…"**

There is a RESTRAINER holding back the revelation of antichrist until he is TAKEN OUT of the WAY. We know what is restraining the antichrist. It is the Church, empowered by the Holy Spirit. This Restrainer is 2-fold in nature, which is why it is called a WHAT in v6 (the Church) and a HE in v7 (the Holy Spirit). So the removal of the Restrainer is the Rapture, the Departure of the Church in v3, our gathering together unto Him (v1). When the Church is taken out of the way, then evil can come to its fullness, especially in the person of the antichrist. God allows it in order to judge it. So the Church is restraining the antichrist until it is taken out of the way and then the antichrist will be revealed. That is why he said in v3 that the departure of the Church must happen first, before the Tribulation begins and the antichrist is revealed.

Paul does not directly identify the Restrainer by name, which means it must be obvious from the context, as good communication requires. Other theories such as the Restrainer being human government have little basis in the context. Remember from v1 that the main subject of the whole passage is the Rapture, the 'taking away' of the Church from the earth. Therefore, when v6-7 talk about the Restrainer being taken out of the way, it must refer to the Church. This makes perfect sense for the Church is God's agent in the earth set in opposition to the spirit of antichrist and holding it back. By definition the spirit of antichrist tries to oppose, deny and replace the truth of Christ. It is the Church that is called to proclaim and exalt Christ, in direct opposition to the spirit of antichrist. Moreover if the Restrainer is not the Church, and its removal is not the Rapture, we have an oddity, in that Paul introduces the Rapture in v1 as the main subject under discussion, and then fails to mention it again, or even allude to it. This is clearly impossible, so the Rapture must be a central feature of the whole passage. When the 'Departure' is seen to be the Rapture, the whole passage fits together perfectly.

So what restrains the antichrist now is the Church, or more precisely the Holy Spirit through the Church. That's why the Restrainer is described as both a WHAT in v6 and a HE in v7. When the Church is removed then the restraining ministry of the Spirit through the Church will also cease. However, the Spirit is omnipresent God and so will continue to be present on the earth, enabling many to get saved in the Tribulation. These verses fit perfectly with v3, which said that the Departure of the Church must happen first and then the antichrist will be revealed. v7-8 says that the Restrainer must be taken out of the way first and then the antichrist will be revealed. Both verses talk about the removal of something and in both cases the result of this removal is the revelation of the antichrist. So they must be talking about the same event. In other words the Departure of the Church from the earth is the same as the Taking away of the Restrainer.

Paul's logic is now clear. First he said that the antichrist cannot be revealed until the Church is removed in the Rapture (v3), then he explained why this was the case. The Church functions as the Restrainer, holding back the revelation of antichrist, so he can only be revealed once the Church is taken out of the way (v6-8). Once the removal of the Restrainer is identified as the Rapture of the Church, then everything fits together perfectly, and it becomes clear this passage teaches a Pre-Tribulation Rapture. Any interpretation of this passage should be tested against v1, which says **the Rapture is the main subject**. Alternative explanations don't even mention the Rapture after v1, showing that something is wrong.

The passage finishes by describing antichrist's destruction at the Second Coming of Christ, v8: **"Then that lawless one will be revealed whom the Lord will slay with the breath of His mouth and bring to an end by the Appearance of His Coming."**

# *Chapter 4: The Rapture in the Book of Revelation

## The Morning Star

We now go on to the teaching of Peter and see that he also taught a Pre-Tribulation Rapture. He speaks of the Morning Star - which is a wonderful picture of the Rapture. 2Peter 1:19: **"We have (1) the PROPHETIC WORD confirmed, which you do well to heed as a light that shines in a dark place, UNTIL (2) the DAY DAWNS, and (3) the MORNING STAR arises in your hearts."**

This describes 3 Lights or Manifestations of Christ.

(1) In this present time we have His Light shining in our hearts through the Prophetic Word. If we are living by the Light of God's Word, we will not walk in darkness. Peter says we must live by this Word: **"UNTIL (2) the DAY dawns, and (3) the MORNING STAR rises in your heart."** This speaks of 2 different future manifestations of Christ's Glory, which compared to 2 natural lights, which are associated with the dawn of a new day. The DAY dawns at SUNRISE when the SUN appears and lights up the whole world. This is a picture of the manifestation of Christ in His 2nd Coming, when He will rise upon the whole world, and all shall see Him in His Glory. Malachi 4:2 describes the Return of Christ as the rising of the SUN of Righteousness covering the whole earth with His Glory (see also Hosea 6:3). His glory will shine outwardly and visibly, bringing a new DAY (the Millennium).

But shortly before the Dawn, while it's still dark, another light rises into view called the MORNING STAR. It is actually the planet Venus (or Sirius), which appears as one of the brightest stars, and is a Sign heralding the coming Dawn. Its appearance means the sun will soon rise and the new Day begin. It only appears to those who are awake and watching. Thus it is a manifestation to true believers only. All will see the Sun, but only some will see the Morning Star. Christ will arise and shine from within their hearts. Those who are not ready to see the Morning Star will miss it. After the appearance of the Morning Star the world remains in darkness for a short time before the Sun rises and all is revealed. The Morning Star is the Sign that the Sun (Jesus) is about to come and bring a new Day when all shall see Him in His glory

In Revelation 22:16, Jesus said: **"I AM the Bright Morning Star."** So the Morning Star is a Manifestation of the Glory of Jesus. Also in Revelation 2:28

Jesus promised believers: **"I will give him the Morning Star."** So this is a special future manifestation of the glory of Jesus that's only given to believers. These are 'romantic' words of love, for He is saying, as the Bridegroom to the Bride: "I will give you MYSELF, I will fill you with My glory."

Also notice that Peter says: **"the Morning Star will arise in your hearts"**, that is, in the hearts of believers. This is different from the Glory of Christ covering the earth at the 2nd Coming. This is a manifestation of Christ's Glory that originates in the hearts of believers. So while the world is asleep in the darkness before Sunrise, when all will see Christ's Glory, there will be a special manifestation of His Glory given to believers only. He will appear to them as 'the Morning Star' and His Glory will arise in their hearts.

**So the Morning Star is the promise of the Glory of Christ manifested to and in believers in the Rapture, before the 2nd Coming.**

This tells us that at the moment of the Rapture, the Glory of Christ will shine in our hearts. It will be manifested within us, and shine out of us. So at the Rapture, Jesus will release His Glory and resurrection power from within (**"Christ in us, the hope of Glory"**) which will transform our bodies and we rise to meet Him! His glory will be revealed in and through us, so that it arises in our hearts, transforming us. The same power that raised Jesus from the dead, the Holy Spirit, is already in our spirit, and on that day Jesus will give the command releasing the Morning Star Glory to surge out of our spirits, through our hearts, then transforming our mortal bodies into immortal bodies. This is the manifestation of the Morning Star. It will happen for us in the Rapture, and 7 years later the new Day will dawn on the earth when the Glory of Christ will cover the whole earth.

### The Book of Revelation

John in the Book of Revelation also teaches the Pre-Tribulation Rapture. In Revelation 1:19 Jesus gave John an outline of the whole Book:

(1) **"Write the things which you have seen"** = the vision of Christ in chapter 1.

(2) **"and the things which are** (now)**"** = the Church-Age in chapters 2-3, described by His 7 letters to the 7 churches (see also Appendix 2).

(3) **"and the things which will take place AFTER this** (after the Church Age)**."** These must be the things that will take place after the Church-Age, described in

chapters 4-22, which include the Church in Heaven (chapter 4-5), the Tribulation (6-18), the 2nd Coming (19), the Millennium and final Judgment (20), and the Eternal State (21-22). Now to confirm that the Church Age ends at the end of chapter 3 and the things that take place after the Church Age (including the Tribulation) start in chapter 4, let's go to Revelation 4:1, where John is called up by a Trumpet into Heaven, symbolic of the Rapture of the Church.

Revelation 4:1: **"After these things** (after the 7 letters describing the Church Age) **I looked, and behold, a door standing open in Heaven, and the first voice which I heard was like** (the sound of) **a trumpet speaking with me, saying: "Come up here, and I will show you things which must take place AFTER this."** These words are clearly introducing a new section of the book using the very same phrase as in 1:19, where John is told that He will be shown things that will take place after the Church-Age. Therefore Revelation 4:1 onwards must reveals events that will take place after the Church Age. As we read on we see that Revelation 4-19 describe the events of the Tribulation in great detail from their initiation in chapters 4-5 to their conclusion in chapter 19. Thus the Church-Age ends before the Tribulation begins. This is why Jesus promised in Matthew 28:19-20 that He would be with the Church, as we fulfil His Great Commission, UNTIL the Tribulation (the End of the Age).

Just as the Church Age will end with the Rapture of the Church into Heaven when we will hear the sound of a trumpet and the voice of Jesus calling us up to Himself, in exactly the same way John was raptured (caught up) to Heaven as a type of the Rapture of the Church (4:1). He is taken forward in time to see what happens after the Church-Age ends and observes firsthand the events of the Tribulation from above, just as the raptured Church will. Thus John's Pre-Tribulation Rapture is a type of the Pre-Tribulation Rapture of the Church. Having been on earth as a representative of the Church to receive revelation about the Church in its ministry on earth as Christ's Lampstand and Light (Revelation 2-3), John is then raptured to heaven (4:1) to view the Tribulation from above. Thus the timing of John's 'rapture' in the typology also supports a Pre-Tribulation Rapture. After the completion of the Church Age at the end of Chapter 3, John (as a type of the Church) is raptured to Heaven, and then observes the actions in Heaven (chapters 4-5), which initiate the Tribulation on the earth.

The 7 letters of Revelation 2 and 3 chart the whole course of the Church-Age, and give Christ's guidance, warnings and promises for the believers in the Church-Age. In particular, Revelation 3:10-11 clearly promises the true Church deliverance from the Tribulation by a Pre-Tribulational Rapture: **"Because you have kept My command to persevere, I also will keep you from the hour of trial** (the Tribulation) **which shall come upon the whole world, to test** (all) **those who dwell on the earth. Behold, I am coming quickly!** (the Rapture). **Hold fast what you have, that no one may take your crown** (at the Judgment Seat of Christ for rewards, straight after the Rapture)."** Some say we will go through the Tribulation and here God promises that to protect us while we are in the Tribulation. But many believers will be killed by the antichrist, so I am not sure what kind of protection they are talking about! Notice, He does not just keep us from the Test or Trial in the sense of just protecting us in it. He says He will keep us from the Hour of Trial, from the very time-period itself. This Trial will come upon ALL who dwell upon the earth, so the only way to be delivered from it is to be removed from the earth. He must do this by means of a Pre-Tribulation Rapture. In fact in v11, Jesus confirms He will do this by means of the Rapture. Once the true Church is removed in the Rapture, whatever remains of the professing Church will be unbelievers, that will be part of the harlot. In Revelation 3:16 Jesus says He will totally reject and disown this apostate Church after the Rapture: **"So then, because you are lukewarm, and neither cold nor hot, I will vomit you out of My mouth."** The Lord would not cast out any who belonged to Him, so all true believers must be removed first (in the Rapture).

John sees the Throne of God in Heaven and 24 elders sitting on thrones. v4: **"Around the Throne were 24 thrones, and upon the thrones I saw 24 elders sitting, clothed in white garments, and golden crowns on their heads."** v10: **"the 24 elders will fall down before Him who sits on the throne and will worship Him who lives forever and ever, and will cast their crowns before the Throne."** The presence of these elders proves that Church is already in Heaven before the Tribulation begins, since it is the opening of the Book with 7 Seals in Revelation 5, which initiates the events of the Tribulation on earth.

An elder is a term that always describes a man of maturity and authority. Angels are never called elders. Neither do angels sit on thrones, whereas men do.

Angels are servants, whereas we will reign with Christ and judge angels. So these elders must be men. Eldership is a representative office of the Church for the elders of a local Church represent that whole Church. Likewise these are the chief elders of the universal Church, who must represent the whole Church.

So the fact they are called elders denotes that they represent a larger group of people, by virtue of their spiritual maturity. Their song in Revelation 5:8-10 reveals who this larger group is: **"The 24 elders fell down before the Lamb, having golden vials full of odours, which are the prayers of saints. And they sung a new song saying: "You are worthy to take the Book, and to open its Seals: for you were slain, and have REDEEMED US to God by your blood out of every kindred, tongue, people and nation; and have made US kings and priests to our God, and WE shall reign on the earth."**

Firstly, notice the elders sing about how they have been redeemed by the blood of Christ. Therefore they are redeemed men. Secondly, they represent a larger group of people, who've also been redeemed, and who are from every nation, and who are kings and priests destined to reign on the earth. This is clearly a description of the Church, so these elders must represent the whole Church. So it is fitting that this term is used, for eldership is an established office of leadership in the church. By singing: **"You have redeemed US to God from every tribe"** these elders clearly identify with this larger group and represent them in their worship before God's Throne.

Another confirmation they are men is that they call themselves royal priests, which are men representing other men to God. We even see them acting as priests presenting the prayers of the saints before the throne. Only a human being can truly identify with and represent other men. The fact there are 24 elders points to David's organisation of priests into 24 divisions, with a chief priest over each division (1Chronicles 24). This indicates these elders are the chief priests over a larger royal priesthood. There is no biblical basis for identifying these elders as angels. They are men who represent the Church. Thus the Church (represented by the 24 elders) is present in Heaven, before the Tribulation begins.

Also these elders are REDEEMED, RESURRECTED and REWARDED men. They sing of their completed redemption (spirit, soul and body). They have already been rewarded, being clothed in white, shining ROBES of GLORY, and wearing golden CROWNS (of honour), and sitting on THRONES (positions) of authority (4:4). Overcomers are promised white robes in the resurrection (3:4-5,

19:8,14). Likewise throne-authority is only promised to men, not angels. Again it is promised to overcomers in the resurrection: **"To him who overcomes I will grant to sit with Me on My throne"** (3:21). Also the word 'stephanos' used for their 'crowns' denotes a victor's crown, given as a reward (as in 2:10). Eternal rewards are often described as crowns. Therefore this confirms they are not disembodied spirits, but men who've already been resurrected and passed through the Judgment Seat of Christ, where we'll all receive our rewards. What is true of the 24 elders must be true of the whole Church they represent. So the Church must already be raptured to Heaven at this point, before the Tribulation begins with the breaking of the 7 Seals. Thus the elders represent the whole Church in Heaven, having been raptured and passed through the Judgment Seat of Christ, and received their rewards. Thus, the Church is raptured and rewarded in Revelation 4, even before the Tribulation begins in Revelation 6!

Revelation 6-18 gives a detailed description of the events of the Tribulation on earth, but the Church on earth isn't mentioned once (not surprising since we have just seen her in heaven). Neither is the Church mentioned in any Old Testament prophecies of the Tribulation. Instead the focus is upon Israel. 'Saints' are mentioned, but this is a general term representing believers of all ages, so it is not specific to the Church (it is used many times in the Old Testament). Israel and the Jews are often mentioned, but not the Church. Why? Because she is no longer present! For example, compare: **"He who has an ear, let him hear what the Spirit says to the Churches"** (2:7,11,17, 29, 3:6,13,22) and: **"If anyone has an ear let him hear"** (13:9). Why are the Churches no longer mentioned? You know why! She must be absent from the earth. The absence of the Church in the Tribulation is most clearly seen in Revelation 7, where 144,000 Jewish evangelists, from the 12 tribes are sealed and anointed as God's witnesses (v1-8), to spearhead the Gospel during the Tribulation, resulting in much fruit (v9-14). They are identified as being of ISRAEL by their tribe rather than as a member of the CHURCH. The Church must be absent, to create this vacancy to be filled by Israel. It means that God will no longer be dealing with the Church as His witness and representative on the earth, but that He will turn again to the Nation of Israel. If the Church were present they would be in the Body of Christ, where nationality is not relevant (Galatians 3:28). Their membership of the Church would override and supersede any natural relationships. Why does God have to suddenly anoint a new group of witnesses? Because the Church has now left!

Thus we see Israel taking centre stage again, once the Church has left. This is consistent with other scriptures on the Tribulation in which Israel is the centre of the action. In the Tribulation God will complete His dealings with Israel, bringing her to faith in Christ, so that she can receive the Kingdom at His Return. The Tribulation is essentially Daniel's 70th Week, during which the final 7 years on Israel's clock will run, culminating in her complete restoration in the Kingdom. Daniel 9:24 specifically says that this counting of time relates to Daniel's people, Israel, which is why the Church-Age is not included in the count. Therefore the 70th Week relates to Israel and not the Church. This shifting from Israel to the mainly Gentile Church (in AD 33) and then back again to Israel in the Tribulation is exactly what Romans 11 teaches. Israel's temporary fall led to salvation going to the Gentiles (v11,12,15), and when the fullness of this (mainly) Gentile harvest has come in, then all Israel will be saved (v25-26). Thus after the harvest from the Church-Age has been ingathered at the Rapture, God will turn again to Israel in the Tribulation in order to bring her to repentance and salvation through Christ.

This focus on Israel (rather than the Church) in the Tribulation is not just seen in Revelation 7, but also in Revelation 11, where the 2 witnesses conduct their world-impacting ministry from the Temple Mount in Jerusalem. It is also seen in Revelation 12, which reveals the spiritual warfare in the Tribulation, for the central character under attack from the dragon is the WOMAN who brought forth the Messiah, who is ISRAEL. This attack culminates in the Campaign of Armageddon (Revelation 16-19) where all the nations gather to destroy ISRAEL. Then of course, Christ returns to Jerusalem to save Israel (Zechariah 14:4). In all of this action centred on Israel, there is no mention of the Church on earth.

We only see the Church again in Revelation 19:7-9 just BEFORE the 2nd Coming. And where is the Church then? Not on earth, but in heaven, with Christ, clothed in white shining linen. Now she is called His Wife. Thus the Rapture, Judgment Seat of Christ and Wedding must have already taken place before the 2nd Coming. It cannot be the same event. Then in Revelation 19:11-16, we see His Wife, the Church, return to earth from heaven with Christ at His 2nd Coming, as part of the armies in heaven, following Him and riding on white horses. She is identified by her clothing of shining white linen received at the Judgment Seat (v8).

Thus when Jesus returns to earth, He is already married and He returns with His Wife (the Church) to the Wedding Feast on earth (v9). Thus a period of time must elapse between the Rapture and the 2nd Coming to allow time for the Wedding, including the final Preparation of the Bride at the Judgment Seat, and her Presentation to Christ in glory; as well as for face-to-face time together before they go forth together to the Wedding Feast on earth (the Second Coming).

Then, in Revelation 20:4, after the 2nd Coming of Christ, it says: **"Then I saw thrones, and they sat on them, and judgment was committed to them."** This is the resurrected Church. Then it describes a separate group of believers who had not yet been raised: **"Then I saw the souls of those who had been beheaded for their witness to Jesus and for the Word of God, who had not worshipped the beast or his image, and had not received his mark on their foreheads or on their hands. And they lived and reigned with Christ for 1000 years."**

This describes the resurrection of the Tribulation martyrs, killed by the antichrist in the Tribulation. Now if the Tribulation was just part of the Church-Age and these believers were part of the Church, they would have been resurrected at the same time as the rest of the Church, rather than as a separate group. These Tribulation Martyrs were not part of the Rapture, therefore they must have been saved after the Rapture and then were killed by the antichrist in the Tribulation, which is why they have a separate resurrection from the Church after the Second Coming. This again confirms the Pre-Tribulation Rapture.

Finally, Revelation 20 confirms there will be a literal Kingdom of God on earth for 1000 years, but if all believers are raptured at the 2nd Coming, only unbelievers will be left alive to populate the Millennium. But other scriptures tell us that Jesus will return as the Judge and will remove all unbelievers from the earth to a place of punishment, leaving no one left alive for the Kingdom!

This contradiction is most plain when you consider the Judgment of the Sheep and Goats in Matthew 25:31-46: **"When the Son of Man comes in His Glory** (to the earth), **and all the holy angels with Him, then He will sit on the Throne of His Glory. All the nations** (gentiles) **will be gathered before Him, and He will separate them one from another, as a shepherd divides his sheep** (believers) **from the goats** (unbelievers). **Then the King will say to those on His right hand: 'Come, you blessed of My Father, inherit the Kingdom... Then He** will also say to those on the left hand: 'Depart from Me, you cursed, into the everlasting fire."

v31 is crystal clear that this Judgment takes place at the 2nd Coming, before the Messianic Kingdom. The location of this Judgment must be the earth for Jesus returns to the earth to judge the world. Therefore the Throne that He will sit on is His earthly Throne, the Throne of David in Jerusalem for in the Kingdom He will reign over the earth from Zion. The population on earth at this time clearly consists of both believers (sheep) and unbelievers (goats), but this is impossible if all believers were raptured at the 2nd Coming! Neither can one argue that these sheep became believers after the 2nd Coming, for Jesus pointed to their lifestyle over a period of time as the evidence of their genuine faith. Moreover Scripture warns clearly that men must make their decision before Jesus returns, for after He returns it will be too late.

So a Post-Tribulation Rapture leads to 2 contradictions. First, there will be no sheep left in their natural bodies for this Judgment. Second, not only are there no sheep left to inherit the Kingdom, but in this Judgment Christ will also remove all the goats (unbelievers) from the earth, leaving no one to populate the Millennium! Therefore there must be a significant time between the Rapture of the Church and the 2nd Coming to allow for another significant soul-harvest to produce these surviving sheep at the 2nd Coming. This criterion is only satisfied by a Pre-Tribulation Rapture.

A final observation from Revelation showing that the Tribulation is a distinct period of time from the Church-Age is from the prayers of the martyrs. The first and prototype Martyr of the Church-Age was Stephen, who followed Christ's example of praying for God's mercy and forgiveness upon his murderers, saying: **"Lord, do not charge them with this sin"** (Acts 7:60). This is appropriate since the Church-Age is generally a time of grace, not judgment. However, the prayer of the Tribulation Martyrs is quite different, calling for Judgment to fall on their murderers: **"How long, O Lord, holy and true, until You judge and avenge our blood on those who dwell on the earth?"** (6:10). This again is appropriate since the Tribulation is a time of Divine Judgement.

In conclusion, the Book of Revelation consistently teaches a Pre-Tribulation Rapture.

## *Chapter 5: The Rapture-Tribulation Issue

There are 4 main views on when the Rapture will happen in relation to the 2nd Coming of Christ. Interestingly, the first 3 views all acknowledge the power of the Wrath Argument, that the Church been promised deliverance from Divine Wrath, and so they agree the Church will be raptured before His Wrath is poured out on the earth. But they differ from each other on when God starts to move in Judgement during the Tribulation.

Therefore the first 3 views all see Christ's Coming as being in 2 Phases: First, He will come FOR His Church in the Rapture, and then months or years later, He will come WITH His Church to the earth in power and glory.

This concept of 2 phases is supported by the great differences in the descriptions of the Rapture and 2nd Coming, indicating they are 2 distinct events rather than different aspects of the same event. This is similar to the Old Testament Prophets seeing both the 1st and 2nd Coming of Christ. Often prophecies of the Second Coming come right after prophecies of the first Coming, as if it might all be part of one big event. Nowhere does it explicitly say it is 2 Comings separated by a long time. But now it is obvious to us that the 2 visions are so different they must be 2 separate events.

*Moreover, there are certain aspects that cannot be harmonised unless there are 2 phases to the 2nd Coming, with a significant time-interval in-between.

*1. The description of life before the Rapture as going on normally, compared to the description of life before the 2nd Coming, which is anything but normal. Everyone will be saying: 'ARMA-GEDDON out of here!'

*2. Another difference is that one set of scriptures, which relate to the Rapture, teach imminence, that the Lord could come at any time. However, another set of scriptures which relate to the 2nd Coming, speak of a series of signs that must happen before the Lord can come, contradicting imminence. (We previously saw a clear example of this in Matthew 24). Some prophecies of His Coming say no man will know when it will happen. But anyone living in the last 7 years will be able to predict from the signs the exact day the Lord will return. The only way to reconcile this is by having 2 separate events, the first (the Rapture) being imminent, and the 2nd (the 2nd Coming) not being imminent, but coming after a set of signs (namely, the events of the Tribulation).

*3. When Jesus returns to judge the earth He will remove all the unbelievers from the earth as the Parable of the Tares, the Judgment of the Sheep and Goats, and the Wise and Foolish Virgins makes clear. Now if the Rapture happens at the same time as the 2nd Coming then all the believers will be in their new bodies, leaving no one to populate the Millennium!

*4. A number of important events related to the Church must take place in Heaven after the Rapture but before the 2nd Coming: (1) the Judgment Seat of Christ, followed by (2) our Presentation to Christ as His glorious Bride, followed by (3) the Wedding Ceremony. All points to a significant time interval rather than a simple U-turn in the atmosphere.

## The Pre-Tribulation Rapture View

*The Pre-Tribulation View says the Rapture will be before the 7-year Tribulation. It is the consequence of following the Keys of Bible Prophecy, such as taking the prophetic scriptures literally, seeing the Church-Age as a Mystery that is distinct from Israel, and seeing the whole Tribulation as a special time of Divine Judgment. One major strength of the Pre-Tribulation view is that it is the only view that upholds Imminence, which is a major doctrine of the New Testament.

Imminence says the Lord could suddenly come for us at any time, so we are to look for Him, wait for Him and watch for His Coming, living every day in the expectancy that He could come any time and we will find ourselves standing before Him giving an account for our lives. Therefore this inspires us to holiness and evangelism, because we want to be found in fellowship with Him and faithfully serving Him when He comes, and indeed many New Testament scriptures motivate us using the doctrine of Imminence. None of the other views preserve imminence, because if the Rapture is at the End of the Tribulation then I know that Jesus cannot come for at least 7 years. Likewise if the Rapture is in the Middle of the Tribulation, then He cannot come for at least another 3.5 years.

## The Mid-Tribulation Rapture View

*The Mid-Tribulation View says the Rapture will happen in the middle of the Tribulation. They say that the 1st half of the Tribulation is just the wrath of man and satan, but the wrath of God only happens in the 2nd half of the

Tribulation. There is little positive evidence of a rapture event at Mid-Tribulation. They just point to the catching up of the 2 witnesses at Mid-Tribulation as a symbol of the Rapture of the Church. They also point out that the 7th and last Trumpet in the Book of Revelation is blown at Mid-Tribulation, and that the Rapture happens at the Last Trump, so they deduce that the 7th Trumpet is the Rapture Trump. However, the 7 Trumpets of Revelation are blown by angels and release judgments, whereas the Rapture Trumpet is called the Trump of God, blown by the Lord Himself to call the Church to rise and meet Him in the air.

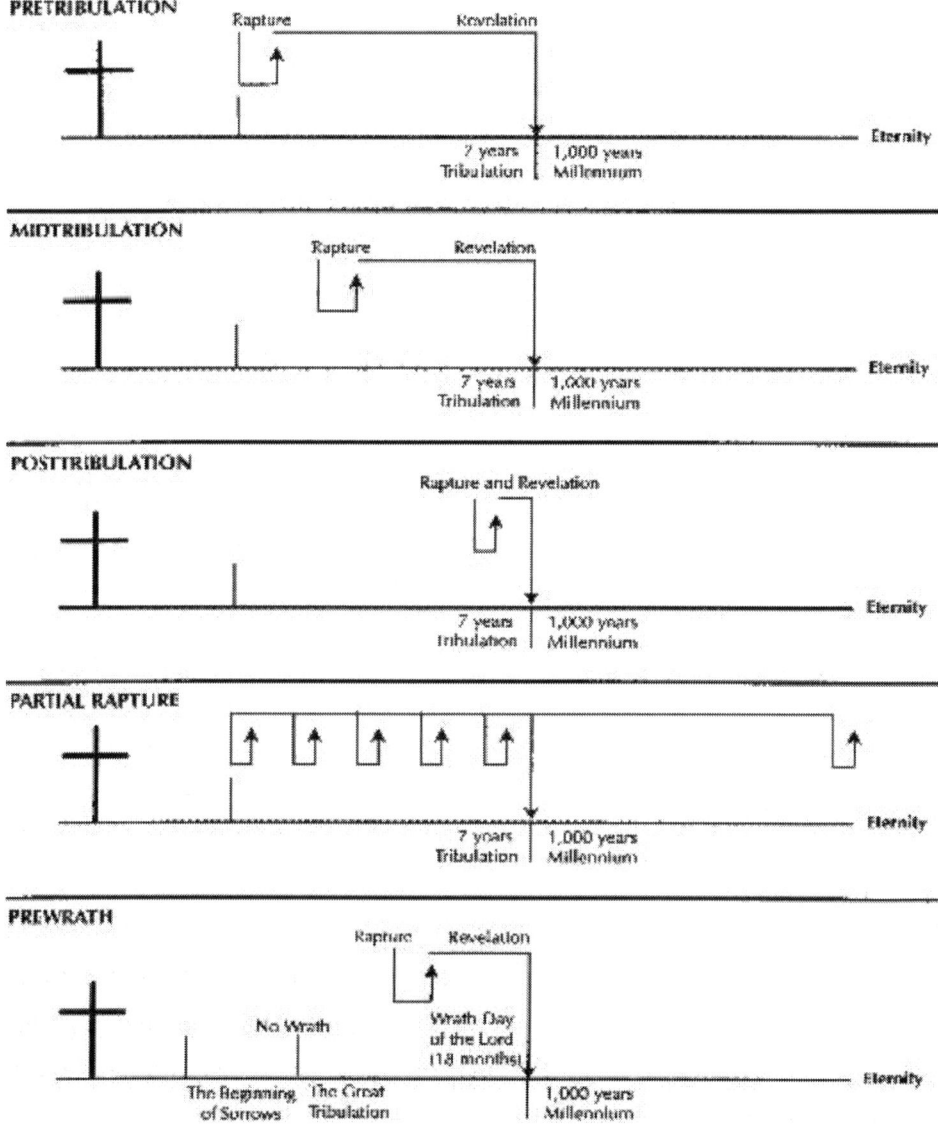

## The Pre-Wrath Rapture View

*The Pre-Wrath View** says the Rapture happens near the end of the Tribulation, but before the 7 Bowls of Wrath, and God only starts moving in judgement when He pours out these Bowls. This is a relatively new view and is quite complex when it comes to understanding all its details. Its key error is in not understanding that the whole of the Tribulation is called 'the Day of the Lord' and that God directly intervenes in judgement right from the start of the Tribulation, so that the whole Tribulation is a time of judgment and not just the final Bowls of Wrath. Revelation is clear that the events on earth in the Tribulation are initiated from heaven by the 7 Seals and 7 Trumpets, as well as the 7 Bowls. In fact, it is Christ who initiates the Tribulation and all its woes by breaking the Seals in Revelation 6. Later when we see the meaning of the Scroll with 7 Seals it will be obvious that Christ is moving forcefully in judgment against the world-system right from the start of the Tribulation.

## The Post-Tribulation Rapture View

*The Post-Tribulation View** says the Rapture and 2nd Coming happen at the same time. As Jesus returns we will rise to meet Him in the air, and then do a U-turn and come back with Him to earth. To support this idea that it is all part of a single event, they give an excellent analogy. In those days when a king came to a city, its leading citizens came out to meet him, and then they would return and enter the city with the king. So this is a picture of going up to meet Jesus in the Rapture and then immediately returning to the earth with Him. But what if the city is in rebellion to the king? Those loyal to the king will go out to greet him, but He will not be able to immediately enter the city. He will have to start a siege to overcome His enemies and forcefully recapture the city, and that is exactly what happens in the Tribulation. We will rise to meet King Jesus in the Rapture, but the world-system rejects Him as King, and so over the next 7 years there is a state of war. When Christ opens the Book, which is the Title Deed of the earth), He is asserting His right as owner to possess the earth and evict the evil tenants. He wages war by withdrawing His mercy (pulling the plug) from the various areas of the world-system, and by releasing direct judgments from heaven (e.g. the Trumpets). This is how to understand the Tribulation and this is why He will withdraw His beloved Bride first.

Now Jesus has the power to destroy His enemies in one day, so why take 7 years before He finally finishes the job at His 2nd Coming? It is because He wants to give them a final chance to be saved. By having 7 years of bombardments, constantly increasing in intensity, He creates the conditions whereby as many as possible can repent and be saved in the Tribulation.

## Further Arguments for the Pre-Tribulation Rapture

We conclude by summarising some of the arguments for the Pre-Tribulation Rapture and explain why this is an important issue with vital practical application for our lives.

**\*1. The Wrath Argument** is based on understanding the nature of the Tribulation as a time of worldwide Divine Judgement or Wrath - which is why it is called 'the Day of the Lord.' This is why Jesus compared the Tribulation to Noah's Flood. Although one characteristic of the whole Tribulation is the wrath of satan and man, with evil coming to fullness, its main characteristic is the Wrath of God, as revealed in the Seal, Trumpet and Bowl Judgments. All the events of the Tribulation are initiated by Christ in Heaven, even from its beginning, when He starts to break the Seals. This can be also seen in the whole structure of Revelation, which constantly switches back and forth between Heaven and earth, showing us that the events (judgments) on earth are initiated from Heaven.

Romans 5:9: **"Much more then, having now been justified by His blood we shall be saved from wrath through Him."** This is not just talking about being saved from Hell, but also from the Wrath of the Tribulation.

When Jesus came the first time He saved us from God's wrath by His death, but 1Thessalonians 1:10 says that when Jesus returns to the earth He does so with the purpose of delivering us (believers) from the Wrath of God coming on the earth: **"We are to wait for His Son to come from Heaven whom He raised from the dead even Jesus, who DELIVERS us from the Wrath to come."** Notice it doesn't say that *He delivered us* from wrath (which He did at the Cross), but that when He returns *He will deliver us* from the coming wrath. This can only mean that He delivers us from the Tribulation (He has already delivered us from Hell), so He will return to deliver the Church from the Tribulation. Later in chapters 4-5 Paul describes how He will do this by the Rapture. He concludes in 1Thessalonians 5:9:

**"God did not appoint us to Wrath but to obtain Salvation** (by the Rapture) **through our Lord Jesus Christ."** Thus our expectation is not the Wrath of the Tribulation, but the Coming of Christ. We are to look for the Rapture not the Tribulation. God has promised the Church in Christ total deliverance from God's wrath (John 5:24, Romans 5:9, 8:1, 1Thessalonians 1:10). Therefore since the Tribulation is a worldwide judgment, He must first remove us from the scene of judgment, namely the earth, just as He removed Noah into the Ark before sending the Flood, just as He removed Lot from Sodom before raining down the fire and brimstone. Thus the principle of God removing believers before judgment is seen in 2 pictures of end-time wrath, which Jesus specifically used to describe to His Coming, comparing it to the days of NOAH and LOT (Luke 17:26-30). In both cases the believers were removed from the scene of judgment to safety before Judgment fell. God always makes a way of escape for believers and since the Tribulation will come upon the whole earth, the only possible escape from it is by the Rapture. Therefore, believers will be removed from the earth before the judgments of the Tribulation fall. We will be removed to safety before judgment falls on them. Would a loving bridegroom subject his bride to His wrath before the wedding? Would Christ subject His own Body (and therefore Himself) to His own wrath? The belief that we need to go through Tribulation-wrath and persecution to be purified is a Protestant Purgatory, which is equally heretical as the Catholic version, in denying the sufficiency of the work of Christ. It would mean that His Blood is not enough! We are purified by His Word, Spirit and Blood not by the antichrist and the Tribulation! And what about those who have died and missed this vital Tribulation-purification?

*2. The AMBASSADORS Argument.** In the Tribulation, God's Kingdom starts waging war on the kingdoms of this world, for He is taking back the earth by force, and by its end He will destroy all earthly kingdoms and establish His Kingdom over all. This is pictured in Daniel 2, which interprets Nebuchadnezzar's dream of a giant statue, representing the main Gentile Powers that dominate Israel. The statue stood until a STONE cut out without hands (representing the Messiah) struck the image on its feet of iron and clay, and broke them in pieces (v34). Then v35 says: **"Then the iron, clay, bronze, silver and gold were crushed together and became like chaff; the wind carried them away so that no trace of them**

**was found. And the stone that struck the image became a great Mountain and filled the whole earth."** This Mountain represents the Messianic Kingdom, according to the interpretation in v44: **"in the days of these kings the God of Heaven will set up a Kingdom which will never be destroyed; it will break in pieces and consume all these kingdoms, and it will stand forever."**

God does not use maximum force and finish the job in 1 day, but spreads the war over 7 years of increasing bombardment to save as many as possible. The Tribulation begins when Christ starts to move against the kingdoms of this world by breaking the Seals. Now when a nation is about to declare war on another nation, it first removes its ambassadors, before hostilities begin. So likewise God will remove His ambassadors before the Tribulation.

### *3. The Psalm 110:1 Argument.

This is confirmed by Psalm 110:1: **"The LORD said to my Lord: "SIT at My right hand, UNTIL I make Your enemies Your footstool."** So Jesus will sit at the Father's right hand UNTIL the time comes for His enemies to be judged and put under His feet. Thus He sits for the duration of the Church Age, but will rise from His Throne to take new action during the Tribulation. The fact He will no longer be permanently seated indicates that He Himself will carry out this judgment, when the Father releases Him. So the action that will signal and initiate a new phase of history when God starts to forcefully put His enemies under foot will be when Jesus rises from His Throne. He will do this when He returns to the earth to fetch His Bride in the Rapture and this will initiate the Tribulation.

It is significant that when Jesus initiates the Judgments of the Tribulation by breaking the Seals, He is STANDING, not SITTING. Revelation 5:5-7: **"Behold the Lion from the tribe of Judah, has overcome so as to open the Book and its 7 Seals ...and I saw in the midst of the throne...a Lamb STANDING...And He came and took the book out of the right hand of Him who sat on the Throne."** The fact that Jesus stands to break the seals at the start of the Tribulation indicates that it is now a new phase of history, where He is no longer sitting. According to Psalm 110 this change of posture means He is now starting to put His enemies under His feet. He is personally starting to take action to intervene in world-events, moving in judgment, for it is the Day of the Lord.

**\*4. The 70 Weeks Argument**. Another reason for the Pre-Tribulation Rapture of the Church comes from Daniel's 70 Weeks, which says that God allocated 490 years on Israel's Clock to fulfil His purposes for Israel. We saw that because Israel rejected the Messiah, God stopped Israel's Clock in AD 33, and brought in the Church as His representatives for the new Church Age, so now God measures time by the Church Clock. But God has not finished with Israel, and there are still 7 years left to run on Israel's Clock by the end of which Israel will be saved and the Messianic Kingdom established (this is the 70th Week). So at some point in the future God will restart Israel's Clock for her last 7 years to run as the Tribulation. During this time of Daniel's 70th Week Israel will again be God's representative and God will fulfil His purposes for Israel. The fact that God will measure time by Israel's Clock in the Tribulation, rather than by the Church's Clock, can only mean that the Church will stop being God's representative on earth. So the Church-Age must end before the Tribulation begins. Thus the Rapture must happen before the Tribulation, so that the baton can be handed back to Israel, for these last 7 years are primarily to do with Israel, as Daniel's 70 Weeks tells us. We see this transfer of anointing back to Israel in the anointing and sealing of the 144,000 Jewish evangelists at the start of the Tribulation. So when the Church Age has finished at the Rapture then God will turn back to Israel and restart her Clock. By the end of these 7 years Israel will fully repent and the Kingdom will be restored to her through the Coming of her Messiah (Daniel 9:24).

From Israel's point of view God inserted the Church Age as a parenthesis within the time of Israel, which delays, but does not cancel God's plans for Israel. It's like a paragraph inserted in a sentence before its end. It doesn't replace or change the main sentence, but delays its end and adds something extra. For example: **"Jim painted the room all morning** (except for a 20 minute tea break) **and finished it at noon."** Likewise: **"ISRAEL** (CHURCH) **ISRAEL."** So Israel has 7 years left to run on her Clock, which can only start again after the Church-Age is finished at the Rapture. Since the Tribulation is part of the time of Israel, the Church-Age must end before it begins (the paragraph must end before the rest of the sentence can resume). When the true Church is raptured (the ingathering of the fullness of the Gentiles), He will graft Israel back in again into the Olive Tree (the place of anointing as His representative) and will complete His plan for her: "all Israel will be saved" (Romans 11:23-27). Thus Israel's clock will restart and the 70th Week will run its course, by the end of which Israel will be fully restored and the Millennial Kingdom established (Daniel 9:24). Those who believe the Church goes through the Tribulation misunderstand the nature of the Tribulation and blur the distinction between Israel and the Church by spiritualising prophecy. The purpose of the Tribulation is to prepare Israel for the Kingdom, and to be a time of worldwide Judgment. Neither purposes have any relation to the Church.

**\*5. A significant interval is needed** between the Rapture and 2nd Coming because the Church in Heaven must go through certain events: \*1. The Judgment Seat. \*2. The Presentation of the Church to Christ. \*3. The Marriage.

**\*6. Millennial Population Argument.** Many scriptures make it clear that Jesus will remove all unbelievers from the earth at His 2nd Coming, so that only believers will enter His Kingdom on earth. But if all the believers are raptured at or near the end of the Tribulation, then there will be nobody left in their natural bodies to populate the Millennial Kingdom on earth! This is a major problem, especially for the Post-Tribulation view, for it will be too late for the unsaved once Jesus returns. Their chance to repent is before He comes again.

(1) Jesus said the Tribulation, which climaxes in the 2nd Coming, will be like the Days of Noah, when all unbelievers were killed, and only the believers were allowed to populate the new earth.

(2) In the Parable of the Tares in Matthew 13:37-43, Jesus made this very point. He compared the world to a field with 2 kinds of seed, the good seed, who are the sons of God; and the tares (the sons of the evil one). In the End of the Age (the Tribulation), which is the harvest time, all tares are gathered and thrown into fire. Thus by the end of the Tribulation all the unsaved will be removed from earth into Hades, so only the righteous by faith will remain to enter the Kingdom.

(3)     Jesus made the same point in Matthew 25:31-46: **"when the Son of Man comes in His glory, and all the angels with Him, then He will sit on His glorious Throne."** This is the Throne of David in Jerusalem from which He will rule over the earth in the Messianic Kingdom. **"All the nations will be gathered before Him; and He will separate them from one another, as the shepherd separates the sheep from the goats; and He will put the sheep on His right, and the goats on the left."** Although it says 'nations' this is primarily a judgment of individuals. This is the word used for Gentiles, so it would better be translated:

**"All the Gentiles will be gathered before Him."** This is a Judgment of all the Gentiles who have survived the Tribulation to determine which of them will be allowed to enter the Messianic Kingdom.

This Judgment is at the 2nd Coming and its location is on the earth, so this is different from the Great White Throne Judgment in Revelation 20, which takes place after the 1000 years. He separates them into 2 groups according to their nature. They are either sheep (believers) or goats (unbelievers).

In v34 He describes the sheep as blessed, that is, they possess eternal life: **"Then the King will say to those on His right: 'Come, you who are BLESSED of My Father, inherit the KINGDOM prepared for you from the foundation of the world."** They inherit the Messianic Kingdom.

But in v41 He describes the goats as accursed, under everlasting damnation: **"Then He will say to those on His left: 'Depart from Me, accursed ones, into the eternal fire which has been prepared for the devil and his angels."** All these unbelievers are removed from the earth to a place of everlasting punishment, first to Hades, to await their Final Judgment in the Lake of Fire. v46 concludes: **"These will go away into eternal punishment, but the righteous into eternal life."** It is clear that no unbelievers who survive the Tribulation will be allowed to remain alive to enter the Messianic Kingdom. Instead they are dismissed to a place of punishment. So only the believers alive at the 2nd Coming will possess the Kingdom.

(4) The Parable of the 10 Virgins (Matthew 25:1-11) teaches the same truth. The 5 who were without oil, who were not born again, at His 2nd Coming, are excluded from the Kingdom. A parallel passage in Matthew 7:21-23 describes Jesus rejecting some who professed faith in Him from entering the Kingdom, on the basis that He never knew them (they were never saved).

(5) We saw that Israel failed to possess the Messianic Kingdom because of unbelief, confirming that the condition to enter the Kingdom is faith in Christ.

Now if the Rapture happens at the 2nd Coming, then as well as all unbelievers being removed by death, all believers will also be removed by Rapture, leaving no one left to populate the Kingdom in their natural bodies. So the Rapture must take place a number of years before the 2nd Coming, in order for there to be enough time to produce a new crop of believers who will populate the Millennium. Only the Pre-Tribulation Rapture fulfils this requirement.

Revelation 7 describes a great soul-harvest in the 1st half of the Tribulation. Soon after the Rapture, God raises up 144,000 Jewish Evangelists who spearhead evangelism in the Tribulation (v1-8), resulting in the salvation of multitudes, seen in v9-17. Many are martyred, especially in the Great Tribulation, but those who endure to the end of the Tribulation will enter the Kingdom, and repopulate the earth. A Mid-Tribulation Rapture does not fulfil the requirement, because at Mid-Tribulation, the Mark of the Beast comes in when everyone will be forced to make their final decision. If they have not been saved by now, they will almost certainly take the Mark to survive, and once they take it they seal their doom forever.

2Thessalonians 2:9-12 confirms the cut-off point for most to receive salvation is at Mid-Tribulation: **"The coming of the lawless one is according to the working of satan, with all power, signs, and lying wonders** (this describes his activity at Mid-Tribulation according to Revelation 13), **and with all unrighteous deception among those who perish, because they did not receive the love of the truth, that they might be saved** (they rejected the Gospel in the 1st half of the Tribulation). **And for this reason God will send them strong delusion** (the mark of the beast), **that they should believe the lie, that they all may be condemned, who did not believe** (love) **the truth but had pleasure in unrighteousness."** So if all believers were raptured at Mid-Tribulation, hardly anyone would be left to populate the Kingdom. But a Pre-Tribulation Rapture followed by a great soul-harvest in the 1st half of the Tribulation, will produce a group of believers who will refuse the Mark and survive to the end.

**\*7. The Blessed Hope Argument.** Many scriptures tell us to HOPE, LOOK, WAIT and WATCH for the personal Coming of the LORD for us, rather than expecting and waiting for the antichrist to kill us. If we were meant to go through the Tribulation, the Church would have been told to prepare and look for the antichrist, for he must come before Christ. But instead we are told to constantly expect and be ready for the Coming of Christ. Therefore, He must come before the Tribulation. 1Thessalonians 1:10 says that we are: **"to WAIT for His Son to come from Heaven whom He raised from the dead even Jesus who delivers us from the Wrath to come** (that is the Tribulation).**"**

Titus 2:13 says we are to be: **"LOOKING for the BLESSED HOPE and Glorious Appearing of our great God and Saviour Jesus Christ."** We are to look for the Blessed Hope of Christ, not the blasted hope of the antichrist! Our focus is to be on the Coming of the Lord - not the antichrist. Our hope is the Appearing of Jesus and our gathering to meet Him at the Rapture. If this is Pre-Tribulation then it is truly a Blessed Hope, but if we must first endure a time of Divine Wrath, and suffering at the hands of antichrist, it would not be such a Blessed Hope! If the Church was going through the Tribulation, we would not have a blessed hope of Christ, but would be looking in fear for the antichrist.

Paul concludes his teaching on the Rapture in 1Thessalonians 4 with the words: **"Therefore COMFORT one another with these words"** (v18). Likewise he concludes his teaching on the Rapture in chapter 5 with the words: **"Therefore, COMFORT each other"** (v11). Thus the primary effect of the true teaching on the Rapture is COMFORT, which encourages us to holiness and evangelism. Now the teaching of the Pre-Tribulation Rapture is obviously comforting for believers, whereas a Post-Tribulation Rapture, which teaches that we must first endure the wrath of satan, antichrist and God, is the opposite. The particular issue faced by the Thessalonians that called forth Paul's comforting teaching on the Rapture, was the death of some of the believers: **"But I do not want you to be ignorant, brethren, concerning those who have fallen asleep, lest you sorrow as others who have no hope"** (4:13). Paul had taught them to live in the imminent expectation of the Rapture, so when some died they sorrowed that these would miss out on this great event, which is why Paul affirmed this was not the case, but that the dead in Christ would rise first (v14-16). This sorrow that Paul addressed is understandable if they were Pre-Tribbers, but if they were Post-Tribbers they would have been glad their loved ones wouldn't have to endure the Tribulation.

**\*8. The Restrainer Argument** (2Thessalonians 2:1-8). Daniel 9:27 and Revelation 6:1 say the Tribulation starts with the revelation of antichrist, making covenant with Israel and going forth in a bid for world-conquest. 2Thessalonians 2:1-3 says that the Day of the Lord (Tribulation) cannot come unless the Departure of the Church in the Rapture happens first (see Appendix 3), and then the antichrist will be revealed (signalling the start of the Tribulation). After describing antichrist's activity at Mid-Tribulation (v4-5), Paul explains why the revelation of the antichrist is so closely linked to the Rapture of the Church, and why he can only be revealed after the Church is removed. There is presently a RESTRAINER holding back the manifestation of antichrist, until he is TAKEN out of the WAY, and then the antichrist will be revealed (v6-8). Remember the subject under discussion is the Rapture - the 'Taking Away' of the Church from the earth (v1). So context demands that the CHURCH, indwelt by the Holy Spirit, is the Restrainer, who will be removed in God's time. Thus the antichrist cannot be revealed (and the Tribulation start) until the one restraining him (the Church) is removed (by the Rapture). This is in perfect harmony with what Paul said in v3 that the Departure (of the Church) must happen before antichrist can be revealed and the Day of the Lord begins. v6-8 repeats the same thought and adds the explanation. Thus a correct interpretation harmonises the whole passage.

The identification of the Restrainer as the Church is evident from other considerations. In the Church-Age, satan has opposed Christ and the Gospel (the spirit of antichrist). He does this by teachings denying the true Christ (His Person and Work). However, satan has not yet achieved his ultimate purpose of manifesting his final antichrist through whom he hopes to rule the world. He wants to use antichrist to completely remove faith in the true Christ. So God's agent in the earth set in opposition to the spirit of antichrist and restraining him is clearly the Church. By the power of the Spirit we are the salt of the earth, restraining corruption. As we use our authority as believers and release God's Word in testimony, preaching, praise, prayer and intercession, the forces of darkness are held back. So, the Church must be removed before evil can come to its fullness and be judged by Christ. Likewise in Revelation, after the Church is taken to heaven, there is a great release of evil on the earth, led by the antichrist.

The Restrainer is described as a 'He' (v7) and an 'it' (v6) indicating a 2-fold activity. The Restraining Ministry is carried out by the Holy Spirit working through the Church. In the Rapture, the Church is removed, but NOT the Holy Spirit, for as God He is omnipresent, and He'll be enabling people to be saved in the Tribulation. Just as the Spirit coming from Heaven to fill the Church in Acts 2 didn't mean He wasn't previously present on the earth, so likewise when the Spirit-indwelt Church is removed from the earth, this doesn't mean the Spirit won't be present on earth anymore. Thus when the Church is removed, although the Spirit is still present, His restraining Ministry through the Church will end.

### *9. The Argument from Imminence

Perhaps the most important reason for believing in the Pre-Tribulation Rapture is that it is the only view that upholds the doctrine of imminence, which has great practical application to our lives. This vital New Testament doctrine says that **the Return of Jesus is imminent** - that is: **He could come AT ANY TIME**. Of course God knows when Jesus will return, but imminence means He has kept this knowledge from us, so that we are to live as if He could come at any time. The Church is told to look for and live in the light of His imminent Coming to translate us into His Presence. Therefore we are to live in constant expectancy, readiness and hope, watching, waiting and looking for His arrival. This blessed hope is a central teaching of the New Testament and is designed to motivate us to holy living and evangelism. It is used many times for this purpose.

For example Hebrews 10:24-25: **"Let us consider one another in order to stir up love and good works, not forsaking the assembling of ourselves together as is the manner of some, but exhorting one another and so much the more as you see the Day approaching."** We need to be in Church, and one key motivation given here is the Lord's imminent Return. Our zeal for God should increase as we see the Day getting closer. This motivates us to be faithful in Church attendance and service. We should run our Christian race every day conscious that at any time soon, we will stand before the Judgment Seat of Christ. This motivation is multiplied when we consider what will happen immediately after the Rapture - namely the Judgment Seat of Christ, when we will all stand before the Lord to give an account for our life and to receive our eternal rewards. Therefore, we should run our Christian race every day conscious that any moment, we will suddenly be raptured and find ourselves standing before the Lord.

Believing in the 'any-moment' Rapture motivates us to get ready and to make the maximum use of the short time remaining. It is NOT a teaching of defeatism and escapism, but creates an urgency and zeal in us to be found holy and occupied in serving the Lord when He returns. There is no doubt that the first generation of Christians lived in the light of the imminent Return of the Lord and that it was a major motivation, enabling them to turn the world upside down. Sadly, as the Church lost hold of the truth of the Pre-Tribulation Rapture, it also lost its vibrant faith in imminence, because the two go hand in hand. Without a belief in the Pre-Tribulation Rapture it's hard to believe in imminence, making it a neglected doctrine in much of the Church. To understand why imminence is only possible with a Pre-Tribulation Rapture, remember that Jesus will return in power and glory at the end of the 7-year Tribulation, which has well-defined Signs marking its start, middle and end. If the Rapture happens at the End of the Tribulation, then imminence is impossible, because it could not happen for at least 7 years. Also anyone in the Tribulation will be able to predict exactly when Jesus returns, since the exact timing of the Tribulation is revealed in Daniel and Revelation. Likewise, if the Rapture was at Mid-Tribulation, then it could not happen for at least 3.5 years. In both cases, a number of Signs must come first, so again imminence is destroyed. Therefore, immanency is only possible with a Pre-Tribulation Rapture, so if we can establish the imminence of the Lord's Return for us, then this would prove the Pre-Tribulation Rapture.

There is in fact overwhelming evidence for Imminence, because the New Testament writers frequently appeal to it to motivate their readers.

### *For example, they describe His Coming as being AT HAND.

Philippians 4:5: **"The Lord is AT HAND."**

1Peter 4:7: **"The end of all things is AT HAND; therefore be serious and watchful in your prayers."**

Revelation 22:7,10: **"Behold I am coming quickly!...for the time is AT HAND."**

James 5:7-9: **"Be patient, brethren, until the COMING of the LORD... Establish your hearts, for the COMING of the LORD is AT HAND. Do not grumble against one another, brethren, lest you be condemned. Behold, the JUDGE is standing AT the DOOR!"**

Romans 13:11: **"Do this knowing the time, that now it is high time to awake out of sleep; for now our salvation** (resurrection) **is nearer than when we first believed. The Night** (the time of being on earth absent from the personal Presence of 'the Sun of Righteousness') **is far spent, the Day** (when we will stand in His glory) **is AT HAND. Therefore let us cast off the works of darkness, and put on the armour of light."**

Revelation starts by saying that the things it reveals: **"must shortly take place"** (1:1), and: **"the time is near"** (1:3), and ends by saying it has revealed: **"the things which must shortly take place"** (22:6).

Twice 1John 2:18 says: **"It is the last hour."**

**\*He is coming QUICKLY**, so we are not to expect any delay. The language of 1Corinthians 15:51-52 describing the Rapture also emphasises its suddenness. Hebrews 10:37: **"For yet a little while, and He who is COMING will COME**

and will NOT DELAY." <u>Revelation 3:11</u>: **"Behold I am COMING QUICKLY** (suddenly)**! Hold fast what you have, that no one take your crown."**

It is particularly impressive that Jesus' final message to us in the final chapter of the Bible is a 3-fold emphasis on His imminent Coming in <u>Revelation 22:7,12,20</u>: **"Behold, I am COMING QUICKLY!... Behold, I am COMING QUICKLY and My reward is with Me to give every one according to his work... Surely I am COMING QUICKLY."** This is sometimes translated as: 'Jesus is coming soon', but literally it means quickly or suddenly, without warning - a plain statement of imminence. Therefore we must remain in a constant state of readiness for His Return, so that we can respond as <u>Revelation 22:7</u> teaches us, by saying to Him: **"Amen. Even so, COME** (now), **Lord Jesus!"**

<u>Jesus Himself taught imminence,</u> when He compared the first phase of His Coming to the coming of a thief (Matthew 24:43-44, Luke 12:39-40, Revelation 3:3, 16:15, 2Peter 3:10, 1Thessalonians 5:1) - a clear statement of imminence. A thief comes suddenly and unannounced, with no warning signs. So His Coming in the Rapture will be unexpected, catching the world off guard and unprepared. He will come, do His work and go away unseen by the unbelievers. The timing is also unknown to believers, but they have been informed about the event, and so if they believe and obey the Scripture they will keep themselves rapture-ready and so not get caught by surprise.

In His description of this dramatic event in the foundational passage in <u>Matthew 24:36-44</u>, His main repeating emphasis is on its imminence.
We see this in <u>v36</u>: **"But of that day and hour** (of His Coming) **no one knows."**
<u>v37-39</u> say there will be no special warning signs beforehand (another indication and proof of imminence), and <u>v40-41</u> emphasise the suddenness of the event.
<u>v42</u> emphasises that even believers don't know the time: **"Watch therefore** (for the Lord, not for Signs), **for you do not know what hour your Lord is coming."**
<u>v43</u> says His Coming will be sudden and without warning, like a thief.  Then
<u>v44</u> totally demolishes any reasonings we may have that Jesus cannot return yet: **"Be ready, for the Son of Man is coming at an hour you do not expect"** (also Luke 12:40).  Also <u>25:13</u>: **"Watch therefore, for you know neither the day nor the hour in which the Son of Man is coming."** Thus Jesus said there will be no specific warning Signs before His Coming in the Rapture, for He would come as a thief, unlike His 2nd Coming in power and manifested glory, which comes after a

whole sequence of well-defined dramatic signs (Matthew 24:7-30). We do not know when the Rapture will be, so we have to always stay ready.

This combination of immanency verses in Matthew 24 answers a perverse interpretation of v36 used by some who want to fix the Rapture to the Feast of Trumpets. They say that this is coded language for the Feast of Trumpets, since it is the only Feast Day on the 1st of a month, and so is determined by the sighting of the new moon. This creates an uncertainty as it could be one of 2 days. Usually the 'Jewish Roots' card is invoked, claiming that any Jew would understand this (beware when people do this, for although there is much value in correctly understanding the true Jewish Roots, they are also often used as a Trojan Horse for false doctrines). It should be obvious that this interpretation of v36 reads ideas into the text that are simply not there. It is perverse, because it reverses the plain meaning that we simply cannot know when Jesus will return for the Rapture. Instead it claims the Rapture can only be on 1 of 2 days every year, and so it cannot be on any of the other days. But this interpretation is contradicted by v44, for if Christ had indeed clearly communicated to them in v36 that they were to expect Him to come at Trumpets, then why did He then say immediately afterwards that He would come at a time when they don't expect Him! Surely Jesus would not make a statement and then contradict it a few verses later.

Imminence is also revealed in the many scriptures that tell us to **WATCH, WAIT and LOOK expectantly for Christ Himself, in His Coming for us.**

The Church is never told to look or watch for the antichrist! We must be always ready, for at any moment we might be caught up to meet the Lord in the air! Some scriptures on watching tell us to look at and discern the Signs of the Times, but their overwhelming emphasis is that we should watch for the Lord Himself, that is, we should live every day with our spiritual focus upon His Return, living in the awareness and eager anticipation that He may come any time, and letting that stimulate and motivate our Christian lives. As a bride waiting for her bridegroom, we wait for Christ knowing our true future and destiny lies with Him.

**\*1. We are to WATCH for His Coming** - not for the Tribulation or the antichrist!: **"WATCH therefore** (get ready, be alert that Jesus is coming soon and live accordingly) **and PRAY always** (do not be spiritually asleep and prayerless)

**that you may be counted worthy to escape** (in the Rapture) **all these things that shall come to pass** (in the Tribulation)**, and to stand** (resurrected) **before the Son of man** (in Heaven - by means of the Rapture)" (Luke 21:36). **"Take heed** (be alert) **WATCH and pray for you know not what hour your Lord shall come"** (Mark 13:33). See also Luke 12:37-40, Mark 13:33-37, Revelation 3:3, 16:15, 1Thessalonians 5:6.

*2. We are to WAIT expectantly for His Coming and the Rapture* (not for the antichrist). So we must be always ready for at any moment we might be caught up to meet the Lord in the air! We are to eagerly WAIT and look for His Appearing at the Rapture: **"Christ was offered once to bear the sins of many. To those who eagerly WAIT for Him, He will appear a second time, apart from sin, for salvation** (of the body)" (Hebrews 9:28). When someone important to us is coming to visit us, during the time we expect his arrival, we wait for him, to be sure we are ready to welcome him. We only wait for him if he could come at that time. If you know he won't arrive until tomorrow, then you won't be waiting for him today. So the fact we are to constantly wait for the Lord to come means that He could come at any time. The fact that this is a central truth for Christian living is seen by the fact that Hebrews 9:28 defines believers as those who are in a state of eagerly waiting for Christ to return. It assumes that this attitude is an intrinsic part of being a Christian.

Our expectation is not the Wrath of the Tribulation, but the Salvation of Christ

1Thessalonians 1:10 tells us that we are: **"to WAIT for His Son** (to come) **from Heaven, whom He raised from the dead** (we await the Rapture)**, even Jesus who delivers** (not delivered) **us from the Wrath** (Tribulation) **to come** (by the Rapture)**."**

The fact that we are WAITING for Jesus to come and rapture us is confirmed by Philippians 3:20-21: **"Our citizenship is in Heaven, from which we also eagerly WAIT for the Saviour, the Lord Jesus Christ, who will transform our lowly body that it may be conformed to His glorious body."**

1Corinthians 1:7-8: **"Eagerly WAITING for the revelation of our Lord Jesus Christ, who will also confirm you to the end, that you may be blameless in the day of our Lord Jesus Christ."**

See also Luke 12:35-36, Romans 8:23, James 5:7.

### *3. We are to LOOK for His Coming, our Blessed Hope.

Titus 2:13: **"We should live soberly, righteously, and godly in the present age, LOOKING for the Blessed Hope and glorious Appearing of our great GOD and SAVIOUR Jesus Christ"** (also Luke 12:46, 21:28, Matthew 24:50, 2Peter 3:12, Jude 21). We are to LOOK for our Blessed Hope - the Appearing of Jesus in the Rapture, not the blasted hope of meeting the antichrist.

To the world, the Rapture will be like a Thief in the Night, removing the Church, but to us it is the coming and appearing of our Bridegroom for His Bride, taking us into the glorious light of His Presence forever (our Blessed Hope). So we are to live eagerly awaiting and preparing for His Return for us. If the Church were going through the Tribulation, we would not be looking for the blessed Appearing of Christ, but instead be looking in fear for the antichrist. We are to look for the Rapture, not the Tribulation. We have the blessed hope of the Rapture, rather than the dread of facing the Tribulation and antichrist. We are to LOOK for the Lord returning as our Bridegroom to take us home (John 14:1-3). So the Church is told to primarily LOOK for the Lord Himself, not for any Signs that must come first (1Thessalonians 5:6-10). This means His Coming must be imminent.

This is why Paul included himself in the 'we' who would be changed, rather than as one of the dead in Christ, who would be raised at the time of the Rapture: **"the dead in Christ will rise first. Then WE who are alive and remain shall be caught up together with them in the clouds to meet the Lord in the air"** (1Thessalonians 4:16,17). **"Behold, I tell you a Mystery: WE shall not all sleep, but WE shall all be changed - in a moment, in the twinkling of an eye, at the last Trumpet. For the Trumpet will sound, and the dead will be raised incorruptible, and WE shall be changed"** (1Corinthians 15:51,52).

Paul wasn't wrong to do this, for in obedience to God he lived in the expectation of the imminent Rapture. So the main focus for our lives now is to be ready for the Coming of our Lord. We need to live in constant hope, looking for His Coming, for at any time, He will suddenly come, without warning, to rapture us.

So our focus (our WATCHING, WAITING and LOOKING) is to be the Coming of the Christ, not of the anti-Christ. This will motivate us to walk before Him in holiness and serve Him zealously with our words and works. For immediately after the Rapture, He will give us a one-on-one interview with a searching examination of our lives, revealing, reviewing and assessing our works and motives, and giving us eternal rewards of glory according to our faithfulness to Him. **Imminence is a powerful motivation spurring us on to live godly lives, to be zealous in evangelism and good works**, so that when He returns, we will receive His commendation and eternal rewards. Many Scriptures motivate us by calling us to live in the light of His imminent Return, urging us to walk in love (1Thessalonians 3:12-13), patience and longsuffering (James 5:8-9), holiness (1John 3:1-3, Titus 2:11-14, I John 2:28, 1Thessalonians 5:23), to faithfully preach the Word and win souls (1Timothy 4:1-2, Jude 21-24. 2Corinthians 5:10-11), to be concerned with heaven and eternity (Colossians 3:1-4), to be steadfast in our labour for the Lord (1Corinthians 15:51-58), faithfully using the gifts that God has given us (1Corinthians 1:7-8), and to refrain from judging others (1Corinthians 4:5, James 5:8-9). The focus for our lives should be the moment we are ruptured and stand before Christ for His approval. But if the emphasis on imminence is removed they lose much of their urgency and motivating power.

Believing in imminence causes us to live our life looking for the Lord (consciously living in the light of His Coming), but if we don't have this belief, we will mostly focus instead on the Signs that must happen first, rather than the Lord's Coming, and this is unbiblical. It isn't a negative teaching of defeatism and escapism. Believing in the 'any-moment' Coming of Christ is a positive and exciting teaching motivating us to get ready and to make the maximum use of the short time remaining. It creates an urgency and zeal to be found holy and busy for the Lord when He returns. The focus for our lives should be that any moment, we will be ruptured and stand before the Lord to give an account for our life.

Now, the Bible's teaching on imminence is undeniable, so often those who reject Pre-Tribulation Rapture try to preserve a watered-down form of imminence, redefining it to mean that for every generation, Jesus could come in their lifetime. So they say that although He could not possibly come in the next few years, because of various events (signs) that must happen first, He could come in our lifetime. However, this does not reflect the immediate urgency of the imminence scriptures, and greatly diminishes their power to motivate us.

For example, imagine you received a letter from the Queen saying that she will pay you a visit any time and will want to tour your house. That would surely motivate you to get yourself and your house ready for inspection, and to stay ready.

But if it said she is coming, but not for a number of years yet, then the impact will be far less. There would be no immediate urgency to change or get ready. Much of the motivating power is lost. Likewise, when imminence is not taught, the church loses its urgency. Thus, one of the main Biblical motivations for godly living has been lost by much of the modern church. This is illustrated in <u>Matthew 24:45-51</u> by the servant who mistreated the other servants because he assumed His Master would delay His Coming. Then he is caught by surprise when the Lord suddenly returns and judges him very strictly. God knows there is something in human nature that slacks off if we think the deadline is a long time away, so He arranged it, so that we must believe He could come at any time.

There are 3 major kinds of motivation for believers in the New Testament based on FAITH, HOPE and LOVE. FAITH is based on the PAST, it says look what God has done for you, and live in the light of that. LOVE speaks of the new nature of Christ in our reborn spirit, and says live in the light of that. HOPE speaks of the future Coming of Christ, which is imminent, and says live in the light of that. Without a vibrant HOPE at best we are only firing on 2 cylinders, but believing in the imminent Rapture will enable us to move up a gear in our Christian life. In Church history when imminence was preached and believed, as in the early church it had the effect of breaking the power of worldliness, and produced increased zeal in evangelism and holiness.

**\*10. The Pre-Tribulation Rapture is consistently taught throughout the New Testament, in (1) the Teaching of Jesus** (Matthew 24:36-44, Luke 21:34-36, John 14:1-3). **(2) the Teaching of Paul** (1Thessalonians 1:10, 4:13-5:11, 2Thessalonians 2:1-12)**, (3) the Teaching of Peter** (2Peter 1:19, Revelation 2:28, 22:16), **(4) the Teaching of John**, throughout the Book of Revelation.

### Objections to the Imminent Pre-Tribulation Rapture

Since the doctrine of Imminence (which requires a Pre-Tribulation Rapture) is such a Biblical doctrine, as well as being exciting and life-changing, it is strange that it is often strongly resisted. One reason might be that it is unsettling, preventing us from being too bound into life in this world. Those focused on this world and this life don't want to hear that at any moment it could all suddenly end, and they will find themselves standing before Jesus having to give an account. This realisation challenges and changes our perspective and priorities and makes us more heavenly minded. It shakes us out of our carnal thinking and complacency into action, because we want the Lord to find us serving Him when He returns. This is why the straw man commonly used by those who this teaching is so misleading. They say that those who believe in the imminent Rapture are escapists, who just want to disengage from this life and bunker down in a holy huddle waiting to be rescued in the Rapture. This is untrue - while it helps us to live with an eternal perspective, with our heart and treasure in heaven, rather than looking to this life alone and its pleasures, it does not create passivity. rather it encourages holiness and good works, especially evangelism, as we want to be found ready. It is true that we want to escape the Divine Wrath of the Tribulation, but we believe it because it is scriptural truth, because Jesus has promised His Church deliverance from wrath, not because of any desire to escape (what we believe will not change what happens, but it dies affect how we live now). The Imminent Coming of the Lord in the Rapture motivates us to live a strong Christian life for the Lord, so it is actually a very positive and practical teaching.

It does create a tension that some do not like, because it stops us from getting too comfortable in this world. Believing Jesus could come any time keeps us looking up and stops us from getting too entangled in the things of this life, but its also possible He will not come for some time, so we also have to live and build our lives accordingly. But we can't get too comfortable here because imminence keeps us on our toes and reminds us this is all temporary. I believe some resist imminence because they do not want to live in this tension. But its healthy for us to remember that our citizenship is in Heaven, and we are just pilgrims here, strangers in a foreign land, ambassadors on assignment, in the world but not of it, so we should not get too attached to it. This was the attitude of the heroes of faith (Hebrews 11:8-10, 13-16). Imminence is good for us spiritually, because it makes us more spiritual-minded, as it focuses us on the Lord Himself (Who is unseen), rather than Signs (which are seen). Many study Bible Prophecy with a carnal mind, with an unhealthy focus on the antichrist and his appearing, being more interested in who he might be, rather than in the Lord's Appearing.

One objection has been, if we are wrong then there will be a lot of people (the 'Pre-Tribbers') who will not be ready to meet the antichrist. First of all, we don't determine truth by weighing the consequences of being wrong and then taking the safe option. We follow where the scriptures lead us, according to literal interpretation. 2nd, there is no special teaching given to the Church to prepare it for the antichrist, apart from the information given in the New Testament about him, so 'Pre-Tribbers', if anything, will be more prepared as generally they are more interested in Bible Prophecy and know these scriptures well. So apart from the initial disappointment at being in the Tribulation they will be no worse off than anyone else. 3rd, there is a far more important meeting that we need to prepare for than any hypothetical meeting with antichrist, and that is our meeting with Christ at the Rapture when our whole life will be reviewed and rewarded. While other teachings focus on getting you ready for the Tribulation and meeting antichrist, the teaching of imminence focuses on getting you ready for your meeting with Christ, and this is surely is more important, and is the right emphasis that's true to the New Testament. Jesus could come at any time and call us to account. So it is vital we prepare ourselves and stay ready for this imminent meeting with Christ, rather than focusing on getting ready for antichrist.

Another objection is based on a misunderstanding of terminology. The most common term used for the final 7 years is the Tribulation, so people compare this to Jesus' words in John 16:33 that: **"in the world you will have tribulation."** Therefore, they deduce (falsely) that it is unscriptural for us to be delivered from the Tribulation. They assume that the Tribulation is just like the Church-Age but a bit worse, not understanding it is completely different in nature (in a few years oat least 4-5 billion will die). Although 'the Tribulation' is a valid and scriptural term, the most common Biblical term is 'the Day of the Lord' signifying it is a time of Divine Judgment. So although it is a time of unprecedented tribulation (trouble) of all sorts, its key aspect is that it is a time of Divine Wrath from which the Church has been promised deliverance. Needless to say the Church has always suffered tribulation and persecution, so the teaching is not about avoiding tribulation, but avoiding the time of Judgment. Some say the Church needs to go through the Tribulation to be purified, a kind of Protestant Purgatory, but what about the majority of the Church over 2000 years, who never got the chance to go through the Tribulation, how will they get purified? My Bible says we are sanctified by the Blood of Jesus, and by the Spirit and Word of God!

I find that many objections to the Pre-Tribulation Rapture are appeals to emotion rather than logic, such as the persecution in China due to communism. Apparently the Chinese converts were taught the Pre-Tribulation Rapture, and on that basis believed they would not suffer persecution, but instead faced horrendous times, which led to a rejection of this teaching. The fact that Corrie ten Boom reported this adds emotional weight. But it should be obvious that either the Pre-Tribulation Rapture was taught wrongly to the Chinese or it was misunderstood, because it does not deny the fact that the Church suffers great persecution at times.

Another kind of emotional objection is particularly objectionable, revealing a kind of desperation in trying to discredit the teaching, rather than just judging it scripturally. I am talking about the attempts to discredit its ORIGINS. The claim is that it is a new doctrine discovered by J.N. Darby 200 years ago. To make matters worse, he got it from some dubious characters (Edward Irving and Margaret Macdonald)! This last accusation involving these 2 characters is mischievous and has now been proven false - Darby came to his conclusions from his own study of the scriptures. In any case we should not give these kind of considerations any weight, because that's not how we decide doctrine. Although the development of doctrine is a worthy study, we don't judge truth by who discovered it, or how recently it was (re)discovered. We judge truth by whether it agrees with the Word or not. Many truths known by the first believers were quickly lost by later generations and only relatively recently rediscovered, as many in the Church turned away from tradition and allegorical interpretation, and turned back to the Bible and its literal interpretation. If we say newly rediscovered truth must be wrong, then we must admit that the Reformers were wrong to teach justification by faith alone. I find it strange that this kind of argument is used against the Pre-Tribulation Rapture, when no one uses it against other doctrines. For example, Covenant Theology is not much older than Dispensationalism, but its relative modernity as a theological system is not used to discredit it, and rightly so.

I will conclude these thoughts by giving a potted history of prophetic doctrine. Obviously we believe the apostles had a clear grasp of the truth, but the early church fathers after them lost a lot of revelation, for example some of them believed in baptismal regeneration. Even so, they believed in a Tribulation, the imminent Coming of Christ and a literal Millennium to follow. They were all clearly Pre-Millennial, but the Tribulation issue is not so clear, as they did not have a developed theology on this issue, as we do today. However, there are early references to a Pre-Tribulation Rapture by the Shepherd of Hermas (95-150 AD), Victorinus, the Bishop of Pettau (270 AD), and Ephrem, the Syrian (306-373 AD) in his 'Sermon on the End of the World' wrote: *"Why therefore do we not reject every care of earthly actions and prepare ourselves for the meeting of the Lord*

*Christ, so that he may draw us from the confusion, which overwhelms all the world? Believe me, dearest brother, because the Coming of the Lord is nigh, believe me, because the end of the world is at hand, believe me, because it is the very last time. Or do you not believe unless you see with your eyes? See to it that this sentence be not fulfilled among you of the prophet who declares: "Woe to those who desire to see the Day of the Lord!" For **all the saints and elect of God are gathered, prior to the Tribulation that is to come, and are taken to the Lord** lest they see the confusion that is to overwhelm the world because of our sins."*

Therefore the doctrine of the Pre-Tribulation Rapture was not unknown before Darby. As Church history went on things got darker, especially as far as prophetic truth is concerned. Allegorical interpretation came in and controlled prophetic interpretation, especially when Augustine endorsed it, resulting in Amillenialism. Even when the Reformers called the Church back to literal interpretation, they broke this rule as far as prophecy was concerned and held to Amillennialism, so the Tribulation issue did not arise. Finally, 200 years ago there was a movement to take the prophetic scriptures literally, which allowed for a systematic study and exciting rediscovery of much truth. Initially, this led to the recovery of Pre-Millennialism as well as the Regathering and Restoration of Israel. Then, literal interpretation also led to the Pre-Tribulation Rapture. At this point we must give Darby credit for being the first to develop a systematic theology based on the literal interpretation of the prophetic scriptures. The truth was there in the Word all the time of course, but the Church did not have eyes to see it, because they did not take the Bible literally in that area. The rediscovery of this prophetic truth, which gained a great acceptance across many churches (not just the Plymouth Brethren, of which Darby was a leader), especially in America, played a large part in helping to motivate the great missionary movements of that time. Moreover, this truth was accepted by the Pentecostal movement 100 years ago and so played a key part in motivating holiness and evangelistic zeal. Another interesting observation is that this doctrinal development of prophetic truth is part of the larger process that's taken place throughout Church history. Church historian James Orr has pointed out that each different period of Church history has seen a different area of doctrine become the focus of attention and controversy, resulting in a systematic study of the scriptures and the development of a systematic theology in that area. The order in which this happened follows the standard order of chapters in any Systematic

Theology book. Appropriately, the last chapter, and the last area to be systematised (in the last 200 years) is Eschatology - the study of last things. So as the Church approached the end-times the Lord has restored understanding of the last things, just when it was most needed, so that we might know the times in which we live. Thus the fact that the Church has finally turned to the serious literal study of prophetic truth is another Sign of being in the end-times, for God told Daniel certain prophetic truths would be sealed until the time of the end, when many would go to and fro through the Bible and as a result prophetic knowledge would increase: **"Daniel, shut up the words, and seal the book until the time of the end; many shall run to and fro, and knowledge shall increase"** (Daniel 12:4).

One reason for this limitation on prophetic revelation was to preserve imminence, for this doctrine says God deliberately limits the prophetic knowledge of each generation, so that from their point of view Jesus could come at any time. So not only do we not know when He will return, but also if we say He can't return now or before a certain time, then we are contradicting His Word. Thus imminence says its God's secret, only He knows when Jesus will return (Matthew 24:36). Thus all we can do is speculate or try to discern it from types and shadows, but we cannot KNOW it, because He has not revealed it by any plain statement of Scripture. Therefore imminence means that in His Sovereignty He reserves the right to break into history at any time, and He says He will do it at a time we do not expect (Matt 24:44) which is a statement designed to confound and humble any human claim of knowing. This statement of Jesus trumps any human reasoning that says Jesus cannot come now. This is the simple answer to the final kind of objection to imminence, which is when people come up with reasons why Jesus cannot come yet, such as He is coming for a glorious Bride and she is not perfect yet. If that is the criteria, the Rapture will never happen, because we live in sinful flesh. The Bride will become perfect and glorious after the Rapture!

Another such argument is that the Gospel has not yet been fully preached to all nations, so Jesus cannot come yet. Now it is a valid motivation for world missions to say, by reaching out we are preparing the way for His Return, but ultimately only God can know and decide when this criteria is met to His satisfaction. It is foolish pride for us to put our reasoning above His plain statements of imminence. Some argue from the viewpoint of our more precise prophetic knowledge (based on the last 200 years of study and on world-events that have now happened), to say Jesus could not have come before 1948 for example, because we understand now that

Israel has to be back in the Land before Daniel's 70th Week begins. The answer is that imminence says that the knowledge of any generation was limited, so that **from their viewpoint** Jesus could come at any time. Also Jesus could have come at any time, because the Rapture is independent of any world-events. Although I believe the Tribulation will start on the day of the Rapture (Matthew 24:38-39, 1Thessalonians 5:2) that fact has rarely been understood. Moreover, there is nothing that says Daniel's 70 Weeks starts straight after the Rapture. In fact, if we knew Israel's covenant with antichrist happened straight after the Rapture that would destroy imminence. We assume it happens soon after, but there is an undefined time between the Rapture and the start of the 70 Weeks (the final 7 years of the Tribulation). Therefore any world event that has taken place before the Rapture (like Israel's Rebirth) could have also happened after it. In this way God has limited our knowledge to humble us and preserve imminence.

Finally, some construct special reasons why imminence was impossible for 1st century believers, for they knew certain prophesied events had to happen first, such as Peter's martyrdom (John 21:18-19) and Jerusalem's destruction prophesied by Jesus (Daniel 9:26, Luke 19:41-44, 21:6,20-24). The answer to the 1st point is that John's Gospel was written AFTER Peter's death, so imminence was preserved. The 2nd point has already been answered by what we said before that the Rapture is not directly tied to the start of the 70th Week, so hypothetically there was an unlimited time for such things to happen after the Rapture. 2ndly, the prophecies of Jerusalem's destruction could have been fulfilled in the Tribulation. Now, we know that is not the case, but the point is that this was a possibility for those living before the destruction (remembering also Revelation had not been written yet). The final answer to all these human reasonings against the plain statements of Scripture is that the 1st century believers, especially Paul, believed in, taught and lived in the light of imminence, and it was one of the keys to their spiritual effectiveness.

### What about Matthew 24:31?

A favorite verse of the Post-Tribulationists is Matthew 24:31 (also Mark 13:27), which describes what Jesus will do after His 2nd Coming (v29.30): **"And He will send His angels with a Great Trumpet, and they will gather together His ELECT** (Israel) **from the 4 winds, from one end of heaven to the other."**

Those who say the Rapture will happen at the end of the Tribulation like to use this verse to support their view. They claim this is a description of the Rapture of the Church, at the same time as the 2$^{nd}$ Coming, but if that were true this verse contradicts their view in which the Rapture happens just before the 2nd Coming (the Church meets the Lord in the air as He is descending to the earth). This view violates the context, which is all about Israel, and we have already established that the elect in this passage must be Israel. Anyone who knows the Old Testament prophets, such as the disciples to whom Jesus was talking, would know He was speaking about the final Regathering of Israel from all nations at Messiah's Coming. He uses the term 'elect' to emphasise her status as His covenant People, and that He is regathering them in fulfilment of His Covenant with them.

The Regathering of Israel is one of the great themes of Bible Prophecy. As well as the initial partial Regathering before the Tribulation, with Israel in unbelief, when the Messiah returns there will be a complete and final regathering of Israel, with her now in faith. This is the subject of a number of Old Testament Prophecies which use **exactly the same language** as Jesus did in <u>Matthew 24:31</u>.

<u>First,</u> the context tells us that the elect in v31 is Israel who are now in faith. We have seen that Jesus will return to save His elect nation Israel at Armageddon, and then will complete the Regathering of Israel in preparation for His Kingdom, in fulfilment of many Old Testament prophecies. The elect here is not the Church, which did not even exist when He spoke these words. The disciples being Jews, who knew their prophets well, would have understood Jesus was talking here about the Regathering of Israel from the nations by the Messiah at His Coming.

<u>Second,</u> **a Great Trumpet** is only mentioned in one other place, <u>Isaiah 27:12-13</u>: **"You will be gathered one by one, O you children of Israel. So it shall be in that day <u>the Great Trumpet</u> will be blown; they will come, who are about to perish in the land of Assyria...and Egypt, and shall worship the Lord in the holy mount at Jerusalem."**

<u>Third,</u> **'the 4 winds of heaven'** is a Hebrew idiom meaning the same as the **'the 4 corners of the earth.'** The prophets often spoke of Israel and other nations being scattered to the 4 winds of heaven (for the Hebrew use of this metaphorical language see Jeremiah 49:32, 36, Ezekiel 5:10,12, Daniel 7:2, 8:8, 11:4, Zechariah

2:6), so this is a prophecy that God will now regather Israel, who had been 'scattered to the 4 winds' (to every nation). Those hearing Jesus' words would have understood His meaning (that He was talking about God regathering Israel to her land), because they knew what this language meant from the Old Testament. Likewise, we need to read the New Testament in light of the Old Testament background and use of language, rather that taking it out of context, and assigning our own meaning to it – namely, that it is talking about the Rapture). The direct link between the scattering of Israel and her Regathering is given in Jeremiah 31:10 **"Hear the word of the LORD, O nations, and declare it in the isles afar off, and say: 'He who SCATTERED Israel will GATHER him, and keep him as a shepherd does his flock."** Many are quick to believe that God scattered them in judgment, but are slow to accept that the same God will regather them in mercy, to fulfil His covenant promises to them.

Other prophecies speak of this final Regathering of Israel in similar ways.

Isaiah 5:26: **"He will lift up a banner to the nations from afar, and will whistle to them** (to Israel) **from the end of the earth; surely they shall come with speed, swiftly."** This is God calling and gathering His people, Israel.

Isaiah 11:11-12: **"On that day** (when the Lord returns to establish His earthly kingdom) **the Lord will again recover the 2nd time with His hand the remnant of His people, who will remain…and He will lift up a standard for the nations and assemble the outcasts of Israel, and gather the dispersed of Judah from the 4 corners of the earth."** See also Zechariah 10:8-10.

So it was prophesied in the Old Testament, using exactly the same language, that when Messiah returns He will blow a Great Trumpet to call his Elect (Israel) to gather them back to their Land. Where is Jesus at this time? From where is He blowing His Trumpet? Israel! So the Trumpet must be gathering people to Israel!

### Partial Rapture?

Finally, we complete our study of the Rapture by asking: "Who will be taken up in the Rapture?" Is it all born-again believers of the Church-Age, or only those who are fully living for the Lord? The Partial Rapture Theory says that not all born-again believers will be raptured, but only the overcomers, those who deserve it. So, only 5 star Christians will go up, and the rest will have to go through the

Tribulation, which will function as a kind of Protestant Purgatory, to complete their sanctification, as they are not yet ready for heaven. Often people who say the Church needs to go through the Tribulation, think this way, believing that the suffering of the Tribulation is necessary to purify the Church, but my Bible says that we are cleansed by the Blood of Christ, and the Word and Spirit of God. You can see how a Partial Rapture makes for a good altar call: *"If you don't get your life straight you'll have to go in the Tribulation and the antichrist will get you. So you better repent."* However, this is not Biblical. It is based on human reasoning. The Rapture is part of our salvation by grace alone, apart from our works. Thus our works do not determine if we qualify to go up in the Rapture. The Rapture is the completion of our salvation - the resurrection of our bodies. In fact if we are in Christ and Christ is in us through the New Birth, when He comes we will automatically be drawn up to meet Him in the air.

This is clearly taught in the main Rapture passage, 1Thessalonians 4:14-17: **"If WE believe that Jesus died and rose again, even so God will bring with Him those who sleep IN JESUS. For this we say to you by the Word of the Lord, that WE who are alive and remain until the Coming of the Lord will by no means precede those who are asleep. For the Lord Himself will descend from heaven with a shout, with the voice of an archangel, and with the trumpet of God. And the dead IN CHRIST will rise first. Then WE who are alive and remain shall be caught up together with them in the clouds to meet the Lord in the air."** Notice that those who are raptured are described as the ones who are alive when He comes, who believe that Jesus died and rose again. Also those who are resurrected at the same time are described as those who sleep IN JESUS, and as the dead IN CHRIST.

In saying: **"the dead IN CHRIST will rise first"**, it is clear that as far as those who have died are concerned, the only qualification for them to rise at this time is that they are IN CHRIST. In this group, some were faithful Christians, but others not so much. But as long as they are in Christ they will be raised at this time. It would be unrighteous of God to use a different criteria for the living believers. This is confirmed by what he says next. Having described the rising up of all the dead in Christ, he says: **"Then WE who are alive and remain will be caught up together with them in the clouds to meet the Lord in the air."** The 'WE who are alive' must also be those who are IN CHRIST, who are alive when the Rapture happens. 1Corinthians 15:51 confirms that all living believers will be raptured: **"Behold, I tell you a Mystery; WE** (believers) **will not all sleep, but WE will ALL be changed."** Will Christ be presented with a disfigured Bride, with an arm, leg and eye and half her teeth missing? I don't think so! The whole body of Christ will rise to meet the Lord in the air.

### Overcomers

The Partial Rapture theory says not all those in Christ will be raptured, but only the overcomers. Now it's true that there are promises given to the overcomers in Revelation 2-3, including the promise of the Morning Star (2:28). So it follows that only the overcomers will make the Rapture.

But what is the Bible definition of an overcomer? Revelation was written by the apostle John, so we should allow John himself to define who is an overcomer. 1John 5:4,5: **"Whatever is born of God overcomes the world; and this is the victory that has overcome the world - our faith. Who is the one who overcomes the world, but he who believes that Jesus is the Son of God?"**

So who is the overcomer? It is the one who is born again, who believes Jesus is the Son of God. So anyone born again is an overcomer. If you have put your trust in Christ, you are an overcomer. You do not have to try and be an overcomer. You are one already! Christ has already overcome the world (John 16:33), and in Him you are more than a conqueror (Romans 8:37). If you are in Christ, then through your union with Christ, all the promises of God are yours in Christ, including the promise of the Rapture (2Corinthians 1:20). To confirm this, if you study all the promises to overcomers in Revelation 2-3 you will discover they are promises given to all believers, and not just to a certain elite group.

The final proof that the partial-rapture theory is wrong is that both Romans 14:10 and 2Corinthians 5:10 say: **"WE** (believers) **shall ALL stand before the Judgment Seat of Christ."** ALL believers from the Church-Age will stand before the Judgment Seat of Christ to give an account and receive their eternal rewards. This will happen soon after the Rapture. Therefore, all true believers in Christ must be raptured together in order to all stand together before Christ.

This answers the main emotional motivation and appeal behind the partial-rapture position, which comes from the feeling that if all believers were in the Rapture, it would be unfair, for surely there should be a difference made between faithful and unfaithful Christians! Indeed there will be a big and eternal difference between believers according to their faithfulness, but this is not manifested in who goes up in the Rapture, but in what happens after the Rapture, at the Judgment Seat, for there we will receive eternal rewards of glory, opportunity and authority, which will differ greatly according to our works in this life. So how we live now is vitally important and will make a big difference to our eternal glory. Those who are lazy, careless servants will deeply regret wasting their time and opportunities, but those who faithfully walk with God and obey Him will be amazed at His generosity on that Day. Thus every blessing of salvation, including our resurrection body at the Rapture, is equally ours on the basis of grace, independent of our works. However, our eternal rewards will be reckoned to us according to our works. We will all have different degrees of reward depending on how we live now, according to our faithfulness to God.

### *Differences between the Rapture and Second Coming of Christ

To summarise our discussion of the Rapture, we list the many differences between the Rapture and 2nd Coming, which mark them out as 2 separate events.

1. **In the Rapture, Christ returns to the AIR.**

   In the 2nd Coming, He comes to the earth.

2. **The Rapture is a joyous reunion.**

   The 2nd Coming brings terrible judgment.

3. **In the Rapture, Jesus coming is seen by believers only.**

   In the 2nd Coming He is seen by all.

4. **In the Rapture, He comes secretly, as a thief in the night.**

   In the 2nd Coming, He comes openly, in manifested power and glory.

5. **In the Rapture, He comes as the BRIDEGROOM.**

   In the 2nd Coming, He comes as the KING of kings and JUDGE of all.

6. **In the Rapture Christ comes FOR His Bride.**

   In the 2nd Coming He comes WITH His Bride.

7. **In the Rapture He removes believers from the earth by translation.**

   In the 2nd Coming He removes unbelievers from the earth by death.

8. **The Rapture brings in the Tribulation - the time of Jacob's Trouble.**

   The 2nd Coming brings in the Millennium - the time of Israel's Restoration.

9. **In the Rapture, He comes as the Morning Star, which is during the night, but it heralds the soon-coming new day, only seen by those watching.**

In the 2nd Coming, He comes as the Sun of Righteousness with healing in His wings, bringing in a new day, the rays of His glory shining upon the whole earth.

10. **The Rapture is IMMINENT and SIGNLESS.**

The 2nd Coming is preceded by many SIGNS.

11. **The Rapture is related to the Church.**

The 2nd Coming is related to Israel and the nations.

12. **The Rapture is a Mystery.**

The 2nd Coming is revealed in Old Testament Prophecy.

13. **At the Rapture, all the believers of the Church-Age will be judged.**

At the 2nd Coming, all the surviving Gentiles will be judged.

14. **After the Rapture, Israel's everlasting Covenants still remain unfulfilled,**

but after the 2nd Coming, they will all be fulfilled.

15. **After the Rapture, the earth will be unchanged,**

but after the 2nd Coming, the earth will be restored.

16. **After the Rapture, evil and the antichrist will be released,**

but at the 2nd Coming, evil and the antichrist will be judged.

17. **The Rapture comes before the Day of the Lord Wrath.**

The 2nd Coming is the climax and conclusion of that Day.

18. **Life before the Rapture will be going on as normal. Men will be saying: "Peace and safety."** But in the Great Tribulation just before the 2nd Coming things on earth will be at their worst ever.

19. **The Rapture is for believers only.** The Second Coming is for all on earth.

20. **The Rapture is the expectation of the Church, our blessed hope of being taken to Heaven.** The 2nd Coming is the expectation of Israel, her earthly hope of inheriting the Messianic Kingdom.

# *Chapter 6: The Judgment Seat of Christ

A missionary came home from the field after many years of faithful work for God. During the voyage he was wondering what kind of welcome he would receive at the dock. As he approached the port there was a cheering crowd and band playing. His spirits were raised. All these had come to greet him. But his face fell as he saw whom they had come to see, for the Prince of Wales had been travelling on the same ship. As he got off he realised there was no welcome for him. In dejection he said to the Lord: "It's not fair. I've laboured and sacrificed for years, but at my homecoming I have nothing." Then the Lord simply said: "This is not your Homecoming." Our true Homecoming is to our true Home (Heaven). The Lord was telling him that his labour was not unseen nor would it be it in vain, for He sees everything we do and He will reward us accordingly, and part of that will be a joyful Homecoming. God does give blessings and rewards in this life, for our faithfulness, but our main payday is yet future at the Judgment Seat of Christ, when we receive our eternal rewards.

All men are created by God and are accountable to God, who is holy and judges us all without partiality and according to truth (Romans 2:2,11), that is, by His absolute moral standards as revealed in His Word, as Jesus said: **"Your Word is truth"** (John 17:17). He does not just look at the outward appearance of what we do, but also at the heart motivation (1Samuel 16:7). Therefore, there will be a time of final judgment for every person.

We have seen that each person's Eternal Judgment happens in **2 Stages**. The **1st Stage, immediately after death, determining our eternal innocence or guilt**, is according to our FAITH - whether or not we have put our trust in Christ alone for our eternal life. We are not saved by our works, but by trusting in Christ and His work for us. Salvation is by grace through faith, independent of our works. Our eternal salvation or condemnation is settled by this judgment. We either stand guilty before God in Adam on the basis of our own works and righteousness, or justified before God in Christ on the basis of His perfect work and righteousness. **The 2nd Stage, which happens immediately after our resurrection, determines either a man's eternal rewards if he has been found righteous, or his eternal punishment if guilty.** In either case the degree of punishment or reward is according to his WORKS. Thus **the 1st Judgement is according to our FAITH and the 2nd Judgment is according to our WORKS.**

In the Bible these 2 issues of faith and works are closely connected. Those who have truly repented and trusted in Christ will start to produce the fruit of good works. Although we have been SAVED from the judgement of our sins through FAITH in Christ, we still have to face the Judgement of our WORKS for our eternal reward. Although we are all equally saved through faith, we will have different degrees of eternal reward depending on our works in this life now.

Those who are alive for the Rapture are a special case, because they do not die, so the 2 Stages happen together. Anyone alive in Christ at that time will be raptured, and immediately find themselves standing before the Judgment Seat of Christ in their new bodies, to give an account to Him of their works, and receive their eternal rewards. This appointment with God will be the most momentous event of your life, an everlasting, irreversible judgment determining your eternal position and degree of glory, and it is imminent. So I must warn you about it, so you can prepare yourself, and make sure you are ready! We need to live our life and run our race with the conscious realisation and expectancy that at any time, we will stand before the Lord to give an account for our Christian life and service to God. This will motivate us to be on fire for God and put His Kingdom first.

### Salvation v Rewards

Some find it hard to reconcile the idea of eternal rewards for our good works with our salvation by grace alone, through faith alone in Christ alone. These are 2 separate issues, which relate to the 2 most important days of your life:

(1) the day you received Christ as your Saviour,

(2) and (2) the day you will stand before His Judgment Seat.

Consider these 5 points of contrast:

*(1) SALVATION is provided for all sinners.** On the other hand, **REWARDS are only awarded to the saints** (believers), God's rightful servants (Rev 11:18).

*(2) SALVATION is the same for all, but REWARDS differ,** because they are proportionate to our acceptable service to God and man: **"The Son of Man will come in the Glory of His Father with His angels, and then He will reward each according to his works"** (Matthew 16:27), **"each one will receive his own reward according to his own labour"** (1Corinthians 3:8). See also Luke 12:47-48

and 2Corinthians 5:10. The Bible encourages us to labour for a 'great reward' (Luke 6:23) or 'full reward' (2John 1:8), so they cannot all be alike: **"Love your enemies, do good, and lend, hoping for nothing in return; and your reward will be great"** (Luke 6:35). To those faithful and courageous under persecution, Jesus said: **"Great is your REWARD in Heaven"** (Matthew 5:12).

**\*(3) SALVATION is God's gracious gift to the lost, but REWARDS are God's gracious wages to the saved**, for their faithful service rendered after salvation, for being a willing and useful servant. **"Behold, I am coming quickly, and My reward is with Me, to give to every one according to his work"** (Rev 22:12). **"He who reaps receives wages, and gathers fruit for eternal life, that both he who sows and he who reaps may rejoice together"** (John 4:36). Whereas we just receive our salvation, we are active participants in earning our reward. Nevertheless these rewards are manifestations of grace, for God does not owe us anything, for when we obey Him, we are only doing what we ought to do. It is His gracious choice, not His obligation, to reward us according to our works. In the Parable in Matthew 20:1-16, a Landowner (a picture of Christ) gave wages to his labourers, above what they deserved. When challenged about this, He justified Himself by asserting His sovereign right to distribute His rewards as He pleases: **"Is it not lawful for me to do what I wish with my own things?"** (v15).

**\*(4) SALVATION is a present possession for believers, but REWARDS are a future possession.** Payment comes after work is done, not before, based on what has been completed satisfactorily. Eternal rewards are awarded only as a result of your service being judged acceptable. This will happen at the Judgment Seat of Christ, which is yet future. Rewards are seen as future: **"If anyone's work which he has built on it endures, he WILL receive a reward"** (1Corinthians 3:14). **"The Crown of Righteousness, which the Lord, the righteous Judge, WILL give to me on that Day"** (2Timothy 4:8). See also Matthew 16:27 and Luke 14:14. Eternal rewards are not to be confused with the temporal blessings and rewards God gives us in this life. These blessings are nothing compared to our future eternal rewards that we will truly possess forever. Rewards are not given until we have run our race in this life and stand in the Presence of our Rewarder.

**\*(5). SALVATION is given on the basis of faith alone, but REWARDS are given on the basis of our works**, the faithfulness of our service to Him. Ephesians

2:8-10 gives the balance between these 2 aspects of faith and works. We are not saved by works (v8-9), but we are saved for works, for the purpose of doing good works (v10), that God might be glorified through our lives, and He chooses to affirm and celebrate these works by graciously crowning them with His eternal glory (our rewards). God has prepared a lifetime of good works for us to walk in and He will reward us according to how faithfully we have walked in His will for us. *"Blood washed believers will be spotless in God's sight, but not all will have the same service record. God is after (willing) obedience. Salvation gets us to Heaven, but works determine what we do after we get there"* (C.S.Lovett).

Ephesians 2:8-10 gives the balance between these 2 issues of (1) salvation by grace through FAITH apart from works, and (2) the importance of GOOD WORKS flowing from our faith: (1) **"By grace you have been saved through faith, and that not of yourselves; it is the gift of God, not of works, lest anyone should boast"** (v8-9). (2) **"For we are His workmanship, created in Christ Jesus for good works, which God prepared beforehand that we should walk in them"** (v10). Although the judgement for believers will be a searching exposure and strict judgment of our works, it will be far better than standing with unbelievers before the Great White Throne (Revelation 20) We will receive eternal rewards, but they will receive their sentencing unto everlasting punishment!

Rewards are often mentioned in Scripture, showing the importance of this subject (Genesis 15:1, Ruth 2:12, 1Samuel 24:19, Psalm 19:9-11, 58:11, Isaiah 62:11, Matthew 5:12, 6:3-4, 10:41, 16:27, Mark 9:41, Colossians 3:23-24, 2John 8). His rewards are a manifestation of His righteousness, love and grace in that it is His way of showing His approval of all that's good and right: **"God is not unjust to forget your work and labour of love which you have shown toward His Name, in that you have ministered to the saints, and do minister"** (Hebrews 6:10). Righteous authorities are like God in both punishing the evildoers and praising (rewarding) those who do good (1Peter 2:14, Romans 13:3-4). Rewards are God's idea, they arise from the heart of God. As fathers love to reward their children from love, and thereby motive them to greater things, so our heavenly Father loves to reward us, and uses His rewards to motive us to excel. He teaches us what He rewards (motives, faith etc.) to motivate these things in us.

## The Timing of this Judgment

The Final Judgment does not happen to all people at the same time, for God judges different groups at different times. For example, the final judgment of believers happens 1000 years before the final judgment of unbelievers. Revelation 20 reveals that the 1st resurrection (of the righteous) takes place before the Millennium but the 2nd resurrection (of the wicked) is after the Millennium. Therefore the final judgment of the righteous, at the Judgment Seat of Christ, takes place at the Rapture and 2nd Coming, but the final judgment of the wicked, at the Great White Throne, takes place 1000 years later. So the judgment of believers for reward takes place before the judgment of unbelievers.

1Peter 4:16-17 confirms this: **"If anyone suffers as a Christian let him not be ashamed, but let him glorify God in this matter. For the time** (is at hand) **for JUDGMENT to begin at the House of God, and if it begins with us first what will be the end of those who do not obey the Gospel of God?"** Suffering believers can rejoice because they will be rewarded at this Judgment for being faithful and courageous under fire. Peter continues in v18: **"Now if the righteous one is scarcely saved, where will the ungodly and sinner appear?"**

## The Judge

As with all judgments the Judge will be the Lord Jesus Christ, who said in John 5:22-23: **"The Father judges no one, but has committed all judgment to the Son, that all should honour the Son just as they honour the Father. He who does not honour the Son does not honour the Father who sent Him."** In v27 Jesus said that the Father: **"has given the Son authority to execute judgment also, because He is the Son of Man."** Because Jesus knows what it is like to live as a man this uniquely qualifies Him to be our judge. In the next verses (28-30), Jesus links this Judgment to the time of the resurrection.

## When?

Next we establish the point that the Judgment for reward of the true Church happens straight after the Rapture. The principle of the Judgement for believers following their Resurrection is clear from Luke 14:14: **"When you give a reception, invite the poor, the crippled, the lame, the blind, and you will be blessed, since they do not have the means to repay you; for you will be REPAID at the RESURRECTION of the RIGHTEOUS."** When we act unselfishly to help those in need, who cannot pay us back, Jesus promises we'll be repaid at the resurrection. This confirms that the judgment for reward for the righteous takes place immediately after their resurrection - for us this means it will be straight after the Rapture of the Church. Likewise, Jesus said in <u>Revelation 22:12</u>: **"Behold, I am COMING quickly, and My REWARD is with Me, to give to every one according to his WORK."** So Jesus will distribute His rewards immediately after He comes in the Rapture.

In <u>Luke 21:36</u> Jesus said that believers who escape the Tribulation in the Rapture will **"STAND before the Son of Man"**, who will be sitting on His Judgment Seat. <u>This will take place in Heaven</u>, for Jesus promised in <u>John 14:1-3</u> that He will return for us in the Rapture and then take us to be with Him in Heaven. This again confirms a Pre-Tribulation Rapture, for in the Post-Tribulation scenario, Jesus raptures us at the 2nd Coming, and we then do a U-turn and return with Him to the earth.

<u>1Corinthians 4:5</u> also confirms this Judgment will be when the Lord comes at the Rapture: **"Judge nothing before the time** (of judgment), **until the Lord comes, Who will bring to light the hidden things of darkness and reveal the counsels** (motives) **of the hearts. Then each one's praise** (reward) **will come from God."** <u>2Timothy 4:1</u>: **"The Lord Jesus Christ will JUDGE the living and the dead: (1) at His Appearing** (the Rapture) **and (2) at His Kingdom** (His 2nd Coming)**."** In view of this Judgement, in v2 he urges ministers to be faithful in preaching the Word. <u>In v8</u>, Paul himself expected to receive a reward on the Day of His Appearing: **"Finally, there is laid up for me the Crown of Righteousness, which the Lord, the righteous Judge, will give to me on that Day, and not to me only but also to all who have loved His Appearing."**

Obviously, only those who are raptured will stand before Christ in this Judgment. So it is a judgment for believers only. It is for all believers of the Church Age, as Paul says: **"Why do you judge your brother? Or why show contempt for your brother? For WE** (brothers and sisters in Christ) **shall ALL stand before the Judgement Seat of Christ"** (Romans 14:10).

This is not a judgment to determine our salvation, for if we have received Christ, we have already been justified and passed from death to life. It is not a judgment of condemnation on our sins, for on the Cross Jesus already paid the penalty and took the judgment for our sins upon Himself, so there is no condemnation for us in Christ. It's not a judgment to determine PUNISHMENT for our sins, but to determine our REWARDS. It is not a judgment to determine if we are SONS of God, but to reward our faithfulness as His SERVANTS. In fact, only the Sons of God will be raptured to stand before the Judgment Seat. It is a judgment of all our WORKS, of our life and service as a Christian, to determine our eternal REWARDS - the glory, honour and authority that we will have throughout eternity. Our capacity for the eternal riches of His glory is determined by our faithfulness to God in this life. So it is not a judgment for punishment, but for reward. Our works will be rewarded, and our reward will determine our eternal capacity for God's glory.

Although God is merciful to forgive us our sins, we should take sin seriously, for it hurts our fellowship with God, and therefore our fruitfulness and eternal reward. But when we confess our sin, He blots it out with His Blood - praise God!    Isaiah 43:25 says: **"I, even I am He Who blots out your transgressions for My own sake and I will remember your sins no more."**

Our life is recorded on God's videotape, so any time out of fellowship is wiped blank and therefore nothing from that time can be presented for a reward. Only what is done in fellowship with God will stand and be rewarded.

Moreover, sin often undermines God's work and testimony, causing others to be discouraged and offended. This undoes the positive effect of your good works for the Lord, and so lessens or even destroys the reward you would have had. If a minister faithfully preaches the Word, but then falls into sin, the fallout will destroy much of the good that he had previously accomplished. As a result he will lose much of his reward, and his lack of faithfulness will disqualify him from opportunities to serve God in a greater way. What God would have entrusted him with, will now be given to another, who will take his crown. When we sin we don't lose our salvation, but we suffer loss of our eternal rewards and that is a serious issue. The subject of rewards is greatly neglected, but it is a major part of the teaching of the New Testament. We need to live our life in the light of the JUDGMENT SEAT of CHRIST.

## The 4 major Passages on this Judgment for Reward

*<u>The first is Romans 14:10-13</u>: **"Why do you judge your brother? Or why do you show contempt for your brother? For we** (believers) **shall all stand before the Judgment Seat of Christ"** (v10). The word for 'Judgment Seat' is the Greek word 'Bema.' It is a high elevated Seat that the Roman Emperor would sit on to render judgment or give out rewards. For example, he sat on a Bema at the Olympic Games, before which the victors stood to receive their rewards (crowns). Likewise after the rapture, Christ will sit on His Judgment Seat and hand out His rewards to us. When we have run our race, we will all stand before the King to receive His rewards, that depend on how well we ran our race in this life, just as Olympians receive gold, silver or bronze medals. In light of this coming judgment, Paul points out that it is foolishness for us to set ourselves up as our brother's judge, since this job belongs to the Lord and He alone is qualified for it. We can judge actions against the Word of God, but we cannot know men's hearts or motives, so we are not qualified to be their judge. If we intrude on His work of judgment, we can expect a strict judgment ourselves. That is why Jesus said. **"Blessed are the merciful, for they shall receive mercy"** (Matthew 5:7), and: **"Judge not lest you be judged. For in the same way you judge others you will be judged and with the measure that use in judging others, it will be measured to you"** (Matthew 7:1,2). Likewise Paul says: **"Who are you to judge another's servant? To his own master he stands or falls"** (Romans 14:4).

<u>Romans 14:11</u>: **"For it is written: "As I live says the Lord, every knee shall bow to Me, and every tongue shall confess to God."** This is a quote from Isaiah 45:23, saying that one day, every man will stand before God and be judged. Paul applies this to the Judgment Seat of Christ, saying that Jesus is the Lord Judge. This proves that Jesus is God, and confirms the Father has given all judgement to His Son. Philippians 2:9-11 confirms Christ will fulfil this prophecy. v12: **"So then each of us** (individually) **shall give an account of himself to God."** In v10 it spoke of the Judgment Seat of Christ, but here it says we give an account to God, again showing that Christ is God).

So you have an appointment with God which you cannot miss. Are you ready? It could happen any time! We will all individually and personally give an account to God for our lives. God, Who sees all, keeps a perfect record of our every thought, word and deed, and will bring our whole Christian life before us, and we will have to give an account for how we have responded to people, situations and God's will. There will be no excuses, or blaming of others in that day, because whatever others do to us, we are responsible for our own actions.

In v13 he concludes: **"Therefore, let us not judge one another anymore, rather resolve not to put a stumbling block in our brother's way."** Rather than focusing on the failings of others we need to watch ourselves and make sure we do not cause others to stumble by our sin and harsh attitudes, and so incur an unfavourable judgment from the Lord on that day. Knowing that soon He will judge us should cause us to focus our attention on ourselves, rather than on others' faults and failings. We need to put all our energy into following God's will for our life, rather than wasting it by judging others. Rather than focusing on others, we need to focus our judging our own attitudes and actions by God's Word, for: **"If we would judge ourselves, we will not be judged"** (1Corinthians 11:31).

Scripture warns us that if we are judgmental against others, God will judge us in a stricter way. James 5:8-9: **"the Coming of the Lord is near. Do not complain, brethren, against one another, so that you yourselves may not be judged; behold, the Judge is standing right at the door!"** Imagine you are one of a group of people about to be judged, and are waiting in the court for the judge, and in his absence you decide to get up and sit in his seat and start to judge and pass out punishments on the others. What will happen when the judge walks in? Who is going to get the strictest judgment? That is why James also said: **"So speak and so act as those who are to be judged by the Law of liberty. For judgment will be merciless to one who has shown no mercy; but mercy triumphs over judgment"** (2:12-13).

Every day has great significance for how you live each day will make a difference to your eternal glory. Your future eternal rewards are at stake. The Judgment Seat of Christ is a strong inducement against sin, especially the sin of judging, which is a proud usurping of the Lord's place, and will result in a great loss of reward. Final judgment belongs to the Lord, so it is wise for us to walk in humility towards others, rather than pride and superiority, for we have such limited knowledge about people's history, situations and motives.

*The 2nd major Passage on Christ's Judgment Seat is 2Corinthians 5:9-11:

**"We make it our aim to be well pleasing to Him... for we** (believers) **must ALL appear before the Judgment Seat of Christ, that each one may receive his reward for the THINGS DONE in the BODY, according to what he has done, whether good or bad."** Again we see this is a judgment for believers only. It is a judgment of our works, 'the things done in the body', in order to determine our reward. It motivates us to live a life pleasing to Him. This will be a thorough searching examination of the quality of all our works, whether good or bad. God sees past the outward action, to the inward thought and motive behind it. Many works that seem good from a human standpoint are in fact they are dead works, done for selfish reasons not from love and faithful obedience to God, works of the flesh, not of the Spirit, to glorify self rather than God. On that day the true quality of all our works will be revealed. Every work is either good or bad, and will either be justified and rewarded, or condemned. Paul concluded in v11: **"Knowing therefore the fear of the Lord, we persuade men."** His awareness that soon he must stand before the Lord, produced in him the Fear of the Lord, motivating him to preach the Gospel and fulfil God's plan for his life.

This Judgment is on all    our WORKS and includes our WORDS. Matthew 12:36,37: **"for EVERY idle WORD men may speak, they will give account of it in the DAY of JUDGMENT.  For by your WORDS you will be justified, and by your WORDS you will be condemned."**

God will reward our WORKS, not our good intentions. As Jesus said, idle, empty words where we promise to do something, but fail to follow through will get no reward, rather they will speak against us. Jesus made this point in Matthew 21:28-30: **"What do you think? A man had 2 sons, and he came to the first and said: "Son, go work today in my vineyard. He answered and said: "I will not", but afterward he regretted it and went. Then he came to the 2nd and said likewise. And he answered and said: "I go, sir", but he didn't go. Which of the 2 did the will of his father?" They said to Him: "The first."**

In evaluating the 7 Churches in Revelation 2-3, Jesus often said: **"I know your works"** (2:2, 2:19, 3:1, 3:8, 3:15). We may say: "He sees my heart." Yes, He does - but we will be judged by what we actually do in loving and serving Him, for this is the ultimate proof of what is in our heart. Jesus said: **"If you love Me, obey**

**my commandments"** (John 14:15). Telling Him we love Him is good, but if we don't prove it by our actions it has little value.

*The 3rd major Passage on Christ's Judgment Seat is 1Corinthians 4:2-5:

**"It is required in stewards** (managers of God's resources) **that one be found FAITHFUL. But with me it is a very small thing that I should be judged by you or by a human court. In fact, I do not even judge myself. For I know nothing against myself, yet I am not justified by this, but He who judges me is the Lord. Therefore judge nothing before the time** (of Judgment), **until the Lord comes, Who will bring to light the hidden things of darkness and reveal the counsels** (motives) **of the hearts. Then each one's praise** (reward) **will come from God."** This passage shows that the quality God is primarily looking for in us is FAITHFULNESS in how we have used the gifts, time, money, energy and opportunities that He has given us, saying: **"It is required that one be found faithful."** It also confirms that: **"He who judges me is the Lord Jesus."** In comparison the judgments of fallible man are of little importance.

Again we see that when God judges, He does not just look at the outward work, but the inner motive behind it, for: **"He will bring to light the hidden things of darkness and reveal the counsels** (secrets) **of the hearts."** The true nature and motive of every work will be revealed, as Jesus said in Luke 8:17: **"Nothing is secret that will not be revealed, nor anything hidden that will not be known and come to light."** Hebrews 4:13: **"There is no creature hidden from His sight, but all things are naked and open to the eyes of Him to Whom we must give account."** God sees and knows everything, even your heart, so you can't hide anything from Him. He will bring everything to the light at the time of this final Judgment: Then: **"each man's praise and reward will come to him from God"** (v5). Again we see that it is a judgment for REWARD, not condemnation, but nevertheless it will be a fearful thing to have our whole life exposed to the light in such a way. But the more we judge ourselves and deal with our bad attitudes now, the less painful and embarrassing it will be for us then.

*The 4th major Passage on the judgment of our works is 1Corinthians 3:10-15 where Paul compares our life to the construction of a building: **"According to the grace of God which was given to me, as a wise master builder I have laid the Foundation and another builds on it. But let each one take heed how he** builds on it. For no other Foundation can anyone lay than that which is already laid, which is Jesus Christ" (v10-11).

Every believer has already received the Foundation on which to build his life, which is the Lord Jesus and His righteousness. This speaks of our salvation by grace through faith in Christ alone. This Foundation was laid by those who preached the Gospel to us. Once we trust in Christ, our life is established on that Foundation. We cannot add anything to this Foundation by our works to secure it, for it is already perfect. This means our salvation is secure, independent of our works. We are not saved by our works, but by the perfect work of Jesus. We must not trust in or build on any other foundation. If we trust in our own works for our salvation then we are building on the wrong foundation and all our works will be worthless and be destroyed, as with the man who build his house on the sand in Matthew 7:24-27. The true Foundation has already been laid when we trusted Christ for our salvation. The issue now is how we build on this Foundation.

v12-14: "Now if anyone builds on this Foundation with gold, silver, precious stones, wood, hay, straw, each one's WORK will become clear; for the DAY (of Judgment) will declare it, because it will be revealed by FIRE; and the fire will test each one's WORK, of what sort (material) it is. If any-one's WORK which he has built on it endures, he will receive a REWARD."

We build upon this Foundation of faith in Christ with our works, and all our works fall into one of 2 categories, they are either: (1) "gold, silver and precious stones", or (2) "wood, hay and straw." The issue is, with what kind of material are we building? At the Judgment Seat, all our works will be tested by the FIRE of God, that burns up everything unworthy. This fire will sweep through the whole of our life, works and ministry, revealing the true nature of every work. It will be a quality test, revealing if it was done in the Lord or in the flesh.

What is the FIRE? Revelation 1:14 says about Jesus: "His head and hair were white like wool as white as snow and HIS EYES like a FLAME of FIRE." Jesus will look into our life with His eyes of flaming fire, with penetrating and consuming insight. His fire will go through our whole life, burning up anything that can be burnt, and what remains of our works, having endured this test of fire, will become the basis of our eternal reward. The nature of fire means this judgment will be thorough, sparing nothing inferior in quality. Only what is of God will remain. The 2 kinds of works will be distinguished by their ability to stand the test of fire. The gold, silver and precious stones will be able to pass through without being consumed. But the wood, hay and straw will be consumed by the fire. Everything of bad quality will be destroyed, for nothing of the flesh can endure in God's Kingdom.

The fire will also purify the works done in God, which please and honour Him. So while some works will be burnt up, other works will be refined and rewarded. One kind of work is indestructible and will endure forever, having eternal value. The other kind is combustible, and will not stand the test of the fire of God's holiness. Thus the QUALITY of our works is more important that the QUANTITY, as everything of inferior quality will be destroyed.

Paul concludes by saying: **"If anyone's WORK is burned, he will suffer loss** (of his reward); **but he himself will be saved, yet so as through fire"** (v15). This proves this is not a judgment of a man's soul but of his works. Even if all his works are burned up, his soul will still be saved, because his salvation does not stand on his works, but on the foundation of Christ and His work. Remember this judgment only concerns those who have already rested their faith on the foundation of Christ. So someone whose life's work is burnt up will suffer loss of reward, but not loss of salvation, which rests on Christ alone. This searching examination will be a very difficult but purifying experience, as the light of Jesus exposes our true motives and reveals our lost opportunities, where what we did for the Lord is measured against what we should have done. There will be weeping in regret before the Lord wipes away our tears.

So there is a future Day of Judgement when the quality of our WORKS will be tested by fire and rewarded. It is not to decide our salvation, but to reveal how well we have built on the foundation of our salvation in Christ. Thus it is a judgment of our works to determine our eternal reward.

### The 3 symbols of good works.

**\*1. GOLD symbolises the DIVINE NATURE.** When we were born again we received the nature of Christ (the fruit of the Spirit) within our spirit. **"God's love has been poured out into our hearts by the Holy Spirit"** (Romans 5:5). So these are works produced from the nature of Christ in us, which we possess through the New Birth. As we walk in the Spirit and Love of God, we produce works of Gold.

On the other hand 1Corinthians 13:3 says: **"If I have not LOVE, what I do profits me nothing."** That is, it brings me no reward.

**\*2. SILVER in the Bible represents REDEMPTION**, so works of silver are works done in grateful response to Christ's redemptive grace, causing us to want to serve Him. They spring from faith in what He has done for us.

**\*3. PRECIOUS STONES** are works of obedience to the commands of God, motivated by a desire to please God and receive His praise and reward, rather than the praise of man. Are we doing what we are doing, because we want men or God to recognise and praise us? If we are just doing it for man's approval, we will stop when no one is looking. But if we do it unto the Lord, to please Him and position ourselves for greater eternal intimacy and glory then we will endure, for we know that He sees all, even if no one else knows. Speaking of the moment of our resurrection when we will be rewarded, 1Corinthians 15:58 says: **"Therefore, my beloved brethren, be steadfast, immovable, always abounding in the work of the Lord, knowing that your labour is not in vain in the Lord."** God sees everything you do and will reward it on that Day.

Both Jesus and Paul said that a defining mark of a believer is that he is motivated by the praise (reward) of God. John 5:44: **"How can you believe, when you receive glory from one another and you do not seek the glory that is from the one and only God?"** Romans 2:29: **"he is a Jew who is one inwardly; and circumcision is that which is of the heart, by the Spirit, not by the letter; and his praise** (reward) **is not from men, but from God."**

**The 3 examples of dead works** (opposites to the 3 kinds of good work).

**\*1. WOOD represents HUMAN FLESH**

These are works done in our own strength and self-will, independently from God. They might look good to man, but are wood.

**\*2. HAY represents human merit**, works done in self-righteousness.

**\*3. STRAW represents human opinion and wisdom**, works that proceed purely from human reasoning, rather than obedience.

Thus we must examine: (1) The POWER energising our works: Are we depending on the power of the Spirit through prayer or on our natural strength (the flesh)? (2) The MOTIVE for our works: Is it love for God and man, from a desire to glorify God? (3) The OBEDIENCE of our works: Do they spring from God's will or are we just following traditions and rituals we happen to like? What a motivation to live for Him now, doing good works of gold, silver and precious stones, and not wasting your life turning out wood, hay and straw!

God sees everything we do and will reward us accordingly: **"God is not unjust to forget your work and labour of love which you have shown toward His Name, in that you have ministered to the saints, and do minister"** (Hebrews 6:10). God does not just see our outward obedience, for He also weighs the heart (Proverbs 21:2, 24:12). **"The Lord does not see as man sees; for man looks at the outward appearance, but the Lord looks at the heart"** (1Samuel 16:7, c.f. 2Corinthians 5:12). **"Whatever you do, do it heartily, as to the Lord and not to men, knowing that from the Lord you will receive the reward of the inheritance; for you serve the Lord Christ. But he who does wrong will be repaid for what he has done, and there is no partiality"** (Colossians 3:23-25). He is looking for willing obedience (from the heart) for it is the willing and obedient who will be rewarded and eat the good of the land (Isaiah 1:18). So walk in fellowship with God, keep short accounts with Him, for any time out of fellowship can't be rewarded. If you sin quickly confess it, and He will forgive and blot out your sin (1John 1:9).

### The 5 Crowns

The eternal REWARDS at the Judgment Seat include 5 CROWNS. The Greek word used for these crowns is 'stephanos', denoting a victor's crown won by athletes in the OLYMPICS. The Crown is given at the end of the race. The Christian life is like running a RACE. So when we have completed our race in this life, we will stand before the Lord and receive our crowns. Jesus said in <u>Revelation 3:10-11</u>: **"I will keep you from the hour of trial which shall come upon the whole world, to test those who dwell on the earth. Behold, I am coming quickly! Hold fast what you have, that no one may take your CROWN!"** This is a promise of Jesus' imminent Return to deliver us from the Tribulation by the Rapture. He confirms that this is the time He will judge and reward us by giving us a crown. He uses this truth to call us to stay faithful, so we do not lose our crown. So God has a crown waiting for you if you are faithful. But if you are unfaithful, you will lose your reward and someone else will get your crown, for doing what you should have done. So hold fast to your calling, walk in fellowship with God, and be faithful.

Let us now look at the 5 kinds of CROWNS we could receive on that Day.

**\*1. The INCORRUPTIBLE CROWN** for walking in the Spirit and not following after the flesh, for exercising self-control and denying yourself in this life, in order to live a Spirit-controlled life, for living in victory over the sin nature. This crown goes to the man who puts God first, rather than the corruptible things of this life. In 1Corinthians 9:24-27 Paul compares him to a disciplined athlete: **"Those who run in a race run to receive the prize** (reward). **Run so to obtain the prize** (the crown)."** We need to have the same determination as Olympic athletes to run our best race and gain the eternal prize at the end of it. **"All who compete** (in the games) **for it** (the prize) **exercise self control in all things"** (v25a). Athletes go into strict training. They cannot just eat and drink anything, and waste their time and expect to win. Their eye is on the prize, so they dedicate themselves to run their best possible race, avoiding distractions and not indulging in things that would slow them down. They exercise dominion over the flesh, denying themselves when necessary. They sacrifice their comfort in the present for a greater and lasting future glory and honour. **"They do it for a perishable CROWN, but we for an IMPERISHABLE** (or incorruptible) **CROWN"** (v25b). The fact that it is incorruptible confirms that this is an eternal reward.

If they exercise self-control and denial for a temporal crown and glory, how much more should we be willing to control our flesh to gain an eternal crown! Whenever we deny ourselves to put the Lord and His work first, or suffer and sacrifice in order to do His will, we are gaining a greater eternal crown of glory, which will far outweigh anything that we have given up in this life.

v26-27: **"Therefore I do not run aimlessly...I discipline my body and bring it into subjection (in order to run with the purpose of fulfilling God's will), lest when I have preached to others I myself should be disqualified."** He is not talking about losing his salvation, but being disqualified from receiving his crown. 2Timothy 2:5 agrees: **"If anyone competes in athletics, he is not CROWNED unless he competes according to the rules."** In those days athletes had to follow strict rules of diet and exercise in their training, otherwise they were disqualified, just as today's athletes are disqualified for taking drugs. Likewise, if we do not do things God's way, but take shortcuts, we will lose our crown.

Paul said that rather than being body-ruled, he brought his body into subjection, so that he would qualify for an eternal crown. To be body-ruled is to dissipate one's life in the various works of the flesh, listed in Galatians 5, including drinking, gambling, sexual sins, strife and worry. The result is disqualification. Paul knew that even he could lose his rewards by letting his flesh rule him. The answer is to be filled with the Spirit and walk in the Spirit every day. We can live a Spirit-filled life, rather than a flesh-controlled life. Then we will gain a Christ-like character, which God will crown with His glory.

Romans 8:1-5 describes how we can walk in the Spirit:

*1. Realise the Mercy of God in Christ has forgiven all your sins and made you right with God (v1): **"There is therefore now no condemnation to those who are in Christ Jesus."**

*2. Realise that your reborn spirit (indwelt) by the Spirit has already overcome sin and death (v2): **"For the law of the Spirit of life in Christ Jesus has made me free from the law of sin and death."**

*3. Realise that on the Cross, Jesus judged and overcame the power of your sin-nature, just as He defeated satan. Therefore although it is still present in your flesh and tries to pull you away from God, it has no authority over you, rather your spirit now has dominion over it, and so you are well able to walk according to the Spirit and overcome it, and so fulfil God's law of love in your life (v3,4): **"For what the law could not do in that it was weak through the flesh, God did by sending His own Son in the likeness of sinful flesh, on account of sin** (our sin-nature in the flesh): **He condemned** (judged and defeated) **sin in the flesh, that the righteous requirement of the law might be fulfilled in us who do not walk according to the flesh but according to the Spirit."**

*4. The key now to walk in the Spirit is simply to set your mind on the things of the Spirit, trusting in His Word and depending on His Power (v5): **"For those who live according to the flesh set their minds on the things of the flesh, but those who live according to the Spirit set their minds on the things of the Spirit."** Galatians 5:16: **"Walk in the spirit and you will not fulfil the lust of the flesh."** In v21 he warns the works of the flesh will cause us to lose our inheritance (rewards) in the Kingdom. Then in v22-23 he describes the qualities of the fruit of the spirit that will be formed in us as we walk in the Spirit. The God will reward such things in us with eternal glory. These things are already in our spirit, but we need to walk in them: **"If we live in the spirit** (that is, if our spirit is alive to God by being born again) **let us also walk in the spirit"** (v25).

## *CROWN 2 - The 'Crown of Rejoicing' or 'Soul-winners Crown.'

1Thessalonians 2:19: **"What is our hope or joy or Crown of Rejoicing? Is it not even YOU in the Presence of our Lord Jesus Christ at His Coming?"** Likewise in Philippians 4:1 Paul called his disciples: **'my JOY and CROWN.'** Again this shows that the Judgment for Reward will happen at His Coming in the Rapture. This Crown of JOY consists of all people we have shared the Gospel with, won to the Lord and discipled: **"He who reaps receives wages, and gathers fruit for eternal life, that both he who sows and he who reaps may rejoice together"** (John 4:36). It will be given to all who fulfil the Great Commission. Thus it is also called the Soul-winner's Crown. We are often too careless and indifferent. God tells us to speak to someone, or pray for them, but we are too busy. We put it off and so souls are lost. It is not enough to be ready for Heaven. We need to take as many as possible with us. We should share our hope with them and invite them to come to Heaven with us.

## *CROWN 3:  The Crown of Righteousness.

At the end of his life, Paul said in 2Timothy 4:7-8: **"I have finished the race, I have kept the faith. Finally there is laid up for me the CROWN of RIGHTEOUSNESS which the Lord will give to me on that Day and not to me only, but also to all who have loved His Appearing."** This Crown is for those who keep the faith, who stay in the truth of God's Word, persevering to the end. They run their race, staying in the right lane, staying in faith and in the will of God, walking in the righteousness until the end. They do this because they love His Appearing. They are focused on the end of the race when they will see the Lord face to face and receive His reward. Paul knew that he was at the point of death and had stayed true to the very end, despite every pressure to turn aside. So he knew he had receive a Crown of Righteousness from the Lord 'on that Day', that is, on the Day of His Appearing to the Church in the Rapture.

In Philippians 3 Paul describes his single-minded attitude as he ran his race keeping his eyes on the prize (eternal reward). In v1-9 he made it clear he was not trust in his own righteousness for salvation but rather in Christ's righteousness. Then in v10-14 he describes his motivation as a Christian: **"that I may know Him** and the power of His resurrection, and the fellowship of His sufferings, being conformed to His death, if, by any means, I may attain to the out-resurrection from the dead (a glorious resurrection in which he would receive great reward) not that I have already attained or am already perfected; but I press on, that I may lay hold of that for which Christ Jesus has also laid hold of me. Brethren, I do not count myself to have apprehended; but one thing I do, forgetting those things which are behind and reaching forward to those things which are ahead, I press toward the goal for the prize of the upward call of God in Christ Jesus (his eternal reward of glory)."

**\*CROWN 4. The Crown of LIFE** given for enduring trials and patience faithfully. James 1:12: **"Blessed is the man who endures temptation** (tests and trials), **for when he has been approved, he will receive the Crown of Life which the Lord has promised to those who love Him"** Rev 2:10: **"Be faithful unto death and I will give you the CROWN of LIFE."** Therefore this Crown is especially for martyrs, those willing to lay their lives down for Him. This Crown is for those who are FAITHFUL to the Lord under testing, who continue to love and trust Him, enduring through trials, temptations and persecutions. If we continue to love Him through sufferings we will receive the Crown of Life. Peter reminds Christians who are suffering for Christ that they will soon stand before His Judgment Seat, so they can rejoice, because they will be rewarded for their faithful witness. Jesus promised those who remained faithful to Him under persecution: **"Blessed are you when men hate you, and when they exclude you, and revile you, and cast out your name as evil, for the Son of Man's sake. Rejoice in that day and leap for joy! For indeed your reward is great in Heaven, for in like manner their fathers did to the prophets"** (Luke 6:22-23).

**\*CROWN 5. The Crown of Glory for faithful leadership and ministry.**
1Peter 5:1-4: **"The elders who are among you I exhort…as a partaker of the GLORY that will be revealed: Shepherd the flock of God which is among you, serving as overseers, not by compulsion but willingly, not for dishonest gain but eagerly; nor as being lords over those entrusted to you, but being examples to the flock; and when the Chief Shepherd appears, you will receive the CROWN of GLORY that does not fade away."**

Jesus will give this Crown of Glory at His Appearing in the Rapture. It is an eternal reward, that 'does not fade away.' It is for elders, and by extension for all who are faithful in positions of leadership, whether in their family, job or ministry. It is for exercising authority in the right way, with a willing and enthusiastic heart, loving, serving and inspiring those under you, setting a good example to them. The greater your faithfulness, the greater your eternal glory.

The more God entrusts to you, the more opportunity you have to prove yourself faithful and qualify for a more glorious crown. But the other side of this is: **"Everyone to whom much is given, from him much will be required, and to whom much has been committed, of him they will ask the more"** (Luke 12:48). As James 3:1 says: **"Not many should desire to be Teachers, for they will face a stricter judgment."** Usually God starts by asking us to be faithful over small things. Be content to be faithful in what God has called you to do, and then as you prove yourself faithful over little, He will entrust you with more.

Luke 16:10: **"He who is faithful in a very little thing is faithful also in much; and he who is unrighteous in a very little thing is unrighteous also in much."** One example of a small thing in which God requires you to be faithful is your money: **"Therefore, if you have not been faithful in the use of unrighteous wealth, who will entrust the true riches to you?"** (v11). The true riches include greater anointing and spiritual authority, as well as eternal rewards. v12: **"And if you have not been faithful in the use of that which is another's, who will give you that which is your own?"** What you possess right now, including your money, is not really your own, because you cannot take it with you to heaven. It belongs to the Lord and is on temporary loan to you to manage. But if you are faithful to use it right, on that basis, He will give you an eternal reward, which will be that which is truly your own, for you will possess it forever.

In Matthew 19:27-30 Jesus described the rewards for those who sacrifice to fulfil God's call on their lives: **"Peter said to Him: "See, we have left all and followed You. Therefore what shall we have (as a reward)?" So Jesus said to them, "Assuredly I say to you, that in the regeneration, when the Son of Man sits on the throne of His glory, you who have followed Me will also sit on 12 thrones, judging the 12 tribes of Israel. Everyone who has left houses or brothers or sisters or father or mother or wife or children or lands, for My**

Name's sake, shall receive a 100-fold, and inherit (more) eternal life (as a reward). **But many who are first will be last, and the last first."**

This last phrase tells us there will be many surprises in that Day. Many outwardly successful ministers will get little reward, because much of what they did was flesh and for their own glory, whereas others who seemed insignificant will receive great reward, because they were faithful in prayer, and in what God told them to do. So do not be jealous of those who seem to be more successful than you. It is unwise to compare your self with others for we all have a different calling (2Corinthians 10:12). Just be faithful with what God gives you to do, and in the end what will matter is your eternal reward.

### Our Eternal Reward consists of the Eternal Glory we will receive

Our present body cannot handle the glory God wants to reveal in us. Only a resurrected body can do this. After standing before the BEMA in our new body and having our works purified by fire, our reward will be given to us by a release of GLORY through us. The Bible says the righteous will shine like the STARS in Heaven (Matthew 13:43), but each star has a different glory. Daniel 12:2-3: **"Multitudes who sleep in the dust of the earth will awake to everlasting life... Those who are wise will shine like the brightness of the heavens, and those who lead many to righteousness like the STARS for ever and ever."** When we are resurrected, we will receive a degree of glory shining out of us, which will differ according to our eternal reward.

1Corinthians 15:40-42 says that in our heavenly resurrection bodies we will be like stars shining with God's glory. Not only will our heavenly body express a far greater glory than our earthly body, but like the stars, we will have different degrees of glory from one another. **"There are heavenly bodies and earthly bodies, but the glory of the heavenly is one, and the glory of the earthly is another. There is one glory of the sun... another glory of the stars; for star differs from star in glory. So also is the resurrection of the dead."** This glory will shine out of us, appearing as white glorious ROBES. It will also crown us. These CROWNS represent our capacity to give glory to God. We will also be given different THRONES of authority to reign with Christ (Revelation 3:21).

The degree of authority and glory we will possess in eternity will be determined by our faithfulness in this life. This should motivates us to follow the

Lord Jesus with all our heart, realising that any moment we will stand before Him to give an account and receive a reward that will be ours forever.

The eternal issue is not just whether we make it to Heaven. It is also how close to God's throne we will be, and how much opportunity, ability and capacity we will have to serve, know, love and glorify God throughout eternity. Our reward in Heaven will be our eternal glory, joy and authority. Much of our reward will be to have a greater capacity for God's life and glory, to have more of God. This depends on how faithful we are in doing God's will in this life, and how much we allow God to mould our character by His Word, and how much we let God's Spirit of love control us and flow through us. The depth of our character determines the amount of GOD'S GLORY we will be able to contain and express in eternity. We will be rewarded with position and glory in Heaven according to the character we have developed and our good works in this life. So what we do now greatly AFFECTS our FUTURE ETERNAL GLORY!

As we walk in the Spirit, there will be sufferings, but as we trust and love God in them, He is able to work a greater glory in us, which will only be manifested when our body is resurrected. Romans 8:17-19: **"If children, then heirs; heirs of God and joint heirs with Christ, if indeed we suffer with Him, that we may also be glorified together. For I consider that the sufferings of this present time are not worthy to be compared with the glory, which shall be revealed in us. For the earnest expectation of the creation eagerly waits for the revealing of the sons of God."** The size of our eternal inheritance depends on our faithfulness to Him in this life. Yes, we will all be perfectly happy and joyful in heaven. All our cups will be full and overflowing with God's life. We will all be filled with God to our full capacity. We will all be shining as stars at maximum strength. However, we will all have different capacities for God's life, joy and glory, depending on how we live now. As we love, trust and obey God, even through suffering, then a greater capacity for His glory is being worked within us. So the depth of our character that we develop now by following Christ determines how much glory we can possess in eternity,

As 2Corinthians 4:17-18 says: **"Our light affliction, which is but for a moment, is working for us a far more exceeding and eternal weight of glory, while we do not look at the things which are seen, but at the things which are** not seen (including our eternal rewards). **For the things which are seen are temporary, but the things which are not seen are eternal."**

Galatians 6:7-10 also uses eternal rewards to motivate us: **"Do not be deceived, God is not mocked; for whatever a man sows, that he will also reap. For he who sows to his flesh will of the flesh reap corruption, but he who sows to the Spirit will of the Spirit reap everlasting life** (a greater abundance of life in eternity). **And let us not grow weary while doing good, for in due season we shall reap if we do not lose heart. Therefore, as we have opportunity, let us do good to all, especially to those who are of the household of faith."**

The choice we face is like choosing £100 now, which just lasts for a week, or having £10,000 next month lasting forever! We can either live unto ourselves now, but have no future reward, or live for the Lord, and later receive a great reward that lasts forever. Of course, our greatest reward will be to know that we have pleased our Lord and helped people. It will be to hear Him say to us: "Well done, good and faithful servant."

### Objections to the teaching of Eternal Rewards

Although the teaching of eternal rewards and their use to motive us is everywhere in the Bible, some have trouble with the teaching of rewards. So we need to deal with some objections. Some think that being motivated by rewards is selfish, that doing things for reward is an invalid motivation, we shouldn't need a reward to do what is right. But this displays a misunderstanding of the nature of eternal rewards. We need to understand that rewards are not like sweeties that are unrelated to what we have done. Rewards are intrinsic to our decisions in this life, not extrinsic and artificial. For example, if your desire, as expressed in your life, is seek the Lord and follow Him and be close to Him and know Him, then your reward will include the fulfilment of that desire, resulting in a special closeness to Him, with a greater opportunity to know Him eternally. If your desire and joy is to serve the Lord and you did that faithfully, then your reward will include greater opportunities to serve Him. If you have been faithful with the authority that He has given you in this life, then your reward will be to be entrusted with greater responsibility and authority to rule for Him. So if your motivation in this life is to glorify God, your reward will be to have a greater ability and glory with which to glorify Him throughout all eternity. Therefore rewards are not selfish, but involve receiving more to use to give to God and others.

Another objection is that rewards are a form of works-righteousness, whereby we earn blessings by our good works, which is incompatible with grace. Indeed it is important to understand that our rewards are not some kind of payment that God is obliged to make for our good works. They are not wages for our good works. Jesus tells a parable about this in Luke 17:7-10: **"Which of you, having a slave ploughing or tending sheep, will say to him when he has come in from the field: "Come immediately and sit down to eat." But will he not say to him: "Prepare something for me to eat, and properly clothe yourself and serve me while I eat and drink; and afterward you may eat and drink. He does not thank the slave because he did the things, which were commanded, does he? So you too, when you do all the things, which are commanded you, say: "We are unworthy slaves; we have done only that which we ought to have done."** That is: 'We have only done our duty'. This word 'unworthy' also translated 'unprofitable', but literally means 'unworthy of any special reward.' Imagine in your job, you faithfully get to work on time and do your hours for a few days, and then you go to the boss and say: '*I have faithfully done my job the last 3 days. You owe me a bonus.'* It would be inappropriate to expect a special reward doing a job you ought to do. Likewise when we serve God with all our heart, we are only doing what we ought to do. He does not owe us any special reward, for He created and saved us. He has done everything for us.

Therefore His rewards are all manifestations of His Grace. They are not what He is obliged to pay us. We do not earn them by our works. So although He chooses to give us rewards for obeying Him, He does not have to do it, so they are all gifts of grace that He chooses to reward us with. Is this why the 24 elders cast their crowns of glory down at Christ's feet (Revelation 4:10)?

### Rewards in the Teaching of Jesus

The final answer to those who object to the idea of eternal rewards, is that our Lord Jesus clearly taught much on the subject of REWARDS and considered it a valid and holy motivation. For example, when Jesus encouraged us to build up our treasures in heaven, He was speaking about our eternal rewards.

Matthew 6:19-21: **"Do not lay up for yourselves treasures on earth, where moth and rust destroy and where thieves break in and steal; but lay up for yourselves treasures** (rewards) **in Heaven, where neither moth nor rust**

**destroys and where thieves do not break in and steal** (they are eternal). **For where your treasure is, there your heart will be also."** If your treasure is your eternal reward in heaven, then your heart will be focused on heaven rather than entangled in the things of this life. It will be set on pleasing God. There are rewards and blessings in this life, but they are temporal and will pass away. Therefore, our most important and valuable treasures are our eternal rewards, which will never pass away and which will never be taken from us. These will only be given to us after this life. So if we have got any sense, we will build up our treasure in heaven by loving and serving God. If our main treasure is in heaven then that is where our heart will be also. In other words, our main motivation and focus will be on pleasing God, and we will put His Kingdom first.

Do not be like the old miser, who at last went to his reward and presented himself at the Pearly Gates, when St.Peter greeted him and escorted him to his new abode. Walking past numerous elegant mansions finally they arrived at a dilapidated shack at the end of the street. Much taken aback, he asked, "Why am I left with a rundown shack when all of these others have fine mansions?" "Well" replied Peter: "we did the best we could with the money you sent us."

In Matthew 6:1-4, Jesus told us not to do our charitable deeds to be seen by man, for then man's praise will be your only reward. Rather do your good work in secret before God, and then He who sees in secret will reward you openly.

Although it will be a thorough and exacting judgment, God will also be generous, rewarding even the smallest act of kindness. Jesus said in Mark 9:41: **"Whoever gives you a cup of water to drink in My Name, because you belong to Christ, assuredly, I say to you, he will by no means lose his reward."** God sees every good work of faith and love you do for Him, and will reward you generously for it with an extra measure of eternal glory. His reward is eternal, and so has infinite value, for it will continue to be ours forever, so whatever we sacrifice will be as nothing in comparison.

### The Parables of Jesus

A number of Jesus' parables give teaching on rewards, for example: The Parable of the Workers in the Vineyard (Matthew 20:1-16), which emphasises they are gifts of God's grace, the Parable of the Rich Fool (Luke 12:13-21), which encourages us to be rich toward God, the Parable of the Unjust Steward (Luke

16:1-13), the Parable of the Minas (Luke 19:11-27) and the Parable of the Talents (Matthew 25:13-30). These all emphasise that God will reward how faithful and generous we have been with the money, gifts, time and strengths He has given us.

The Parables of the Minas and Talents are similar to each other and both depict the Judgment of Christ's servants at His Judgment Seat. In both He compares Himself to a Master who goes away to a far country (Heaven), and entrusts some resources to His servants (believers) to use while He is away. In Luke He gave them all one Mina (100 days wages), whereas in Matthew He gave each of the servants a different amount of Talents (15 years wages). In some ways we have all been given the same New Birth, Holy Spirit, and Word of God. But in other ways we all have different talents, abilities, positions, opportunities and gifts. But everything we have is ultimately His. The question is, are we using what we have to serve Him and forward His Kingdom, or are we just putting it in the ground and not using the opportunities that God has given us? He told them to occupy themselves and use His money (resources) productively. Some were faithful to use that money, but others were lazy and hid it in the ground.

When the Master returned (as He will at the Rapture) He called them to stand before Him to give an account of what they had done with His money. He then rewarded them according to their faithfulness. To the faithful ones He said: **"'Well done, good and faithful servant; you have been faithful over a few things, I will make you ruler over many things. Enter into the joy of your Lord"** (Matthew 25:21,23). So our rewards include an increased joy in His Presence, much of which is through knowing we have pleased Him. What a wonderful thing it would be to receive the Lord's commendation! There are degrees of reward for different degrees of faithfulness for in Luke He made one ruler over 5 cities, and another ruler over 10 cities, since he was twice as fruitful with the same money. This shows that our rewards also include ruling authority.

The principle of being rewarded for our faithfulness, rather than for our gifts, is seen in Matthew, where the 2 servants, one with 5 talents and the other with 2 talents are both equally faithful in doubling their money, and so receive the same reward. Therefore we are not to compare ourselves with others, for we all have different gifts. We are just required to be faithful with what God has given us. One of Jesus' favourite sayings is: **"Many who are first** (in earthly position and gifting) **will be last** (in heavenly reward), **and the last** (in position and gifting) **first** (in reward)" (Matthew 19:30, 20:16, Mark 10:31, Luke 13:30).

Although our good works do not save us, they are nevertheless vitally important in determining our eternal position and state of glory. In this way, God honours us by making us responsible and accountable for our life.

The lazy servants who did nothing with the Master's money were rebuked and suffered a total loss of reward and future opportunities to serve. The Master said: **"Take the talent from him, and give it to him who has 10 talents. For to everyone who has** (faithfulness), **more** (reward) **will be given, and he will have abundance, but from him who does not have** (faithfulness)**, even what he has will be taken away"** (Matthew 25:28-29). They had to go to a place of relative outer darkness further from the throne compared to the brightness of glory where the faithful servants lived. How sad it would be to be rebuked for being a lazy and disobedient servant. These are the ones that do not serve God but just do things that work for their own personal ends, advantage and glory. They will be shown what they should have done and the opportunities they missed because of their unfaithfulness and as a result: **"There will be weeping and gnashing of teeth"** (Matthew 25:30), in great regret as they realise they have suffered loss of eternal reward (1Cor 3:15) and feel deeply how they have failed their Lord. However, in His love the Lord will then wipe away all their tears.

It is significant that the reason for the laziness of this wicked servant was that he did not believe in the doctrine of eternal rewards (Matthew 25:24-26), that the master would not be gracious and generous in rewarding his efforts, and so he did not bother to make an effort or to take a risk or even just to invest the money. Understanding the teaching of rewards is a vital motivation for our life of faith.

Having dealt with His servants (at the Rapture) the Master then slays all His enemies (Luke 19:27). This speaks of His judgment of unbelievers (rebels who do not want Him to reign over them) in the Tribulation and at His 2nd Coming.

Make sure you are ready for this great Day. Remember that at any moment you will have to stand before the Lord and give an account as He reveals your whole life to you and assesses it, before then giving you your eternal reward. Make sure you walk in fellowship with God every day, being zealous for good-works, prayerfully bearing fruit for God. Focus on judging yourself rather than everyone else. Walk in love, and for your own sake repent of those bad attitudes.

## *Appendix 1: The meaning of 'Apostasia' in 2Thessalonians 2

One of the key Rapture passages is 2Thessalonians 2, whose correct interpretation depends on the correct identification of the meaning of **apostasia** in v3: **"Let no one deceive you by any means; for that Day** (the Day of the Lord) **will not come unless THE APOSTASIA comes first, and the man of sin is revealed."** It is often translated FALLING AWAY based on the view that it refers to a religious defection (apostasy) or falling away (departure) from the faith in the last days (c.f. 1Timothy 4:1), after which the antichrist is revealed. This view became dominant through the 1611 King James Version. One problem with this view is that Paul is using *'the apostasia'* as a well-defined sign of a specific event that must happen before the Day of the Lord, as confirmed by the use of the definite article, yet apostasy has always taken place throughout the Age, and Paul does not seem to give any further guidance as to what is special about this unique 'falling away.' Neither are we told elsewhere in the New Testament of a unique end-time event in the form of a special defection from the faith. Some appeal to 1Timothy 4:1ff, but this does not describe a unique event but a growing trend that was already present. Also 2Timothy 3:1ff does not describe an apostasy from the faith, but the increasing lawlessness of evil men in the latter days (see v13). Also 1 and 2 Timothy were written many years after 2 Thessalonians. Therefore there are a number of guesses as to what it is, varying between apostasy in the world, the Church or Israel. Some would prefer to translate it as the Revolt or Rebellion denoting a more forceful rejection of God. Either way it is an unsatisfactory situation as it means that God has provided a Sign, but in such a way that we have no way of knowing for sure what it is, and so can't recognise it when it happens!

Unfortunately the common translation of Apostasia as 'the falling away' or 'the apostasy' feeds in an interpretation that closes the mind to other possibilities. It would be better to translate it as 'the Departure' as the older translations did, as this is the basic meaning of the word. Since Paul did not specify what kind of departure he was talking about (as he did in 1Timothy 4:1 when he said many will **"depart from the faith"**), it would be better to follow suit and leave the possibilities open for now. Translating it as 'the Departure' allows for the meaning of 'Departure from the faith', but it also allows for other possibilities.

For the first 15 centuries translations consistently rendered *apostasia* as 'departure' leaving it open as to what kind of departure was meant (whether a departure from the faith or a spatial departure). The 4th century Latin translation by Jerome (the Vulgate) reflects this standard understanding by using the Latin word *discessio* meaning 'departure.' Thus the earliest English versions used the neutral term 'departure', namely the Wycliffe Bible (1384), Tyndale Bible (1526), Coverdale Bible (1535), Cranmer Bible (1539), Breeches Bible (1576), Beza Bible (1583) and Geneva Bible (1608). Later Beza, a member of the Geneva Bible Translation Committee and disciple of Calvin, was the first to break this trend by transliterating the Greek term *apostasia* which pointed to a religious defection or falling away (apostasy). The fact that *apostasia* is similar to our word 'apostasy' (defection from the truth) is beside the point as we don't interpret Scripture on the basis of a transliterated word to which a certain meaning has been given, but on the basis of what the Greek word meant to the first century reader. Perhaps Beza thought it would help his cause in the theological battle with Romanism, by relating it to the popish apostasy, who he believed was the man of sin. Soon after the King James Version (1611) continued in this direction by translating it 'falling away', and in so doing inserted their interpretation of it rather than giving the basic translation. Since then translations have generally followed the practice of the KJV in not using 'departure', but instead 'rebellion', 'falling away', 'rejection of God', 'great revolt' or 'apostasy.' Had they simply translated the word instead of interpreting it, they would have better rendered it by the word 'departure.'

If we allow that 'apostasia' essentially means 'departure', an alternative view presents itself, which solves all the problems of this passage, and for which I argue in this book, that *the apostasia* in v3 refers to **the Rapture, the Departure of the Church from the earth,** before the Day of the Lord (Tribulation) begins with the revelation of the man of sin. If this is true then this passage clearly teaches the Pre-Tribulation Rapture, and so it is understandable why many would resist this interpretation. However, sadly, even among Pre-Tribulationists this is a minority view. This is unfortunate for, as I will endeavour to show, the case for identifying *the apostasia* as the Rapture is stronger than is generally realised. The most well known proponents for this view are E.Schuyler English, Kenneth Wuest, Thomas Ice and Wayne House. Those who have argued against it include Robert Gundry, Paul Feinberg and William Combs. In this chapter, I summarise the evidence in these previous works, and point to a piece of evidence that has not been mentioned yet in the debate, and introduce a new line of argument, which tips things firmly in favour of the *apostasia* in 2Thessalonians being the Rapture.

### Word meanings

First we need to determine the semantic range of possible meanings for this word to see if 'apostasia' can mean a physical, spatial departure as well as a spiritual departure. In so doing, we will point to vital evidence that has been overlooked in previous discussions. Then we will apply the law of context to determine the specific meaning of *apostasia* in this passage. If the noun *apostasía* can refer to a physical departure, then the context of 2Thessalonians 2 strongly points to Paul using this word to describe the Rapture. To decide if a physical departure is a possibility it is necessary to study the possible range of meanings of the word *apostasia*, gathering evidence from its etymology (roots), history and usage.

*The associated (root) verbal form** from which the noun *apostasia* is derived is *aphistamai* (the present middle of *aphistemi*). The simple verb *histemi* means "to stand," the prefix *apo* means "off, away from," and the compound verb, "to stand off from" denoting a departing to a distance, a separating apart. The word does not mean "to fall" (as in 'falling away') which would be the word *pipto*. Thayer defines it as: *"to make stand off, cause to withdraw, to stand off, stand aloof, to desert, to withdraw from one"; in contexts where a defection from the faith is in view, it means "to fall away, become faithless."* The verb *aphistemi* is clearly used of physical departure in both Testaments. In the Septuagint (LXX) it is used in Genesis 12:8 of Abram's departure from Shechem toward the hills east of Bethel, of David's departure from Saul (1Samuel 18:13), and the physical separation of the wicked from God's presence (Psalm 6:8). The use of the verbal form in the LXX is primarily used for a spatial departure. In the New Testament there are clear examples of the use of the verb to express physical departure or separation. Luke 2:37 says Anna never left the temple, and in Acts 19:9 Paul taught in the synagogue in Ephesus for 3 months before departing when they rejected him. In this case, as in many others the physical departure has a spiritual basis, so the word may carry both aspects (that is, we should beware of overdoing the Greek thinking that separates the physical and spiritual as either/or, when often both may be involved). The KJV translates it 'to depart' (Luke 2:37; 4:13; 13:27; Acts 12:10; 15:38; 19:9; 22:29; 2Cor 12:8; 1Tim 4:1; 2Tim 2:19; Heb 3:12), 'withdraw' (1Tim 6:5), 'fall away' (Luke 8:13), 'drew away' (Acts 5:37) and 'refrain' (Acts 5:38). So it is used 15 times in the New Testament, of which only 3 have anything to do with a spiritual departure from the faith (Luke 8:13, 1Tim 4:1, Heb 3:12). So the predominant translation of the verbal form is 'to depart', and when it is translated differently, the context adds the idea of 'falling away' to the verb, which action is still a departure. In most cases, a physical departure is primarily in view. So the verb often means to physically depart in both the Greek Old and New Testaments, and this departing may be good or bad from the perspective of the writer. So we would expect this basic meaning of the verb to carry over to the associated noun.

The standard response to this evidence is that it does not necessarily follow that the related noun form (cognate) should carry the meaning of the verb (that is, the idea of spatial separation), although both counterexamples that Feinberg produces fail upon closer inspection ('ana' also means 'again', and 'eperotema' does actually mean 'request' and is best translated as such in 1Peter 3:21). A 3rd example used is another cognate noun from this verb meaning 'divorce', which they say is a 'relational separation.' But does not divorce also include the idea of physical separation? To 'send her away' is as much a physical as relational act. In reality, in many 'departures' both spiritual and physical elements are present together. So it won't do to just plead the 'root fallacy' and use it to dismiss all evidence of this nature. It may not be conclusive in itself, but it is certainly good evidence in favour of this position, which should be taken into account even if cognates do not provide absolute proof. If the verb form primarily means spatial separation then that at least creates a presumption that the noun includes that idea within its range of meanings, even if it is not a winning argument in itself. So the verb is a valid help in helping to establish the meaning of derivative nouns.

From this verb are derived 4 nouns. Compared to the large number of uses of the verb in the literature, there are relatively few uses of the 4 related nouns: (1) *Apostasion* (masc) is found with a fixed meaning in both Testaments, related to the breaking of the marriage covenant (Mal 2:14), and means 'a certificate of divorce' (Deut 24:1,3; Isaiah 50:1; Jer 3:8; Matt 5:31; 19:7, Mark 10:4), which results in physical separation. (2) *apostates* - a rebel or deserter, someone who separates himself physically from a group he was in due to differences of belief, (3) the other cognate *apostasia* (fem) is the word we are studying. So far we have seen that the primary use of the verbal form (root) is to describe a physical departure in a general sense, and is by no means limited to a specialised meaning of rebelling against God or forsaking the faith. Therefore we would expect this to transfer to the related noun, at least as a possible meaning. Since a noun takes its meaning from the verb, the noun is likely to have a similar semantic range as their cognate verbs. In most cases the meaning of the underlying verb carries over to its derivative noun. Generally nouns and verbs stay within the same field of usage, so nouns participate in the meaning of their root verb (this is true as a rule, even if there are exceptions). So the Complete Biblical Library says: "its (*aphistemi's*) meanings of 'go away' and 'depart' can also be applied to *apostasia* to give a secondary meaning of removal or departure." (4) *apostasis* is an earlier form of *apostasia* that was used in classical times, and it includes 'physical departure' among its meanings, which implies *apostasia* can probably have this meaning also, based on its origins.

Obviously we must also study a noun's own usage to fully establish its meaning. We will see that this actually supports the evidence from the verb, for although the majority of the uses of the noun *apostasia* in the literature emphasise the spiritual aspect, it did sometimes carry the idea of spatial departure, and this is true for the classical, koine and patristic eras. Considering the mere handful of uses of *apostasia* we have in the literature, it's significant that we can still find evidence of its spatial use in each era, establishing the fact that although it is a secondary meaning, it is within the semantic range of the word, and therefore if it is the meaning that makes best sense from the context, it is the correct meaning.

So now we go on to the usage of the noun *apostasía* in each of the 3 eras.

*For the Classical Period*, the LSJ (Liddell-Scott-Jones Lexicon), the primary Greek-English Classical Lexicon, says *apostasia* is a late form for *apostasis* and gives the following meanings for *apostasia/apostasis*: 1. defection, revolt, esp. in a religious sense, rebellion against God, apostasy, **2. departure, disappearance**, 3. distinguishing, **4. distance.** Thus it gives spatial departure and distance (separation) as secondary meanings, indicating that the meaning of 'spatial departure' can be found in classical Greek. Although *apostasia* as such does not occur in the classical period, it is a later construction of *apostasis* (and so is essentially the same word), which was used of spatial departure in classical Greek.

*The evidence used from the Koine period* (from Alexander the Great through New Testament times) is used by opponents of the *apostasia* Rapture, as the proof positive for their view, claiming that in the koine period no example of spatial departure or separation is to be found. However, this is incorrect, as is the assertion that *apostasia* first occurs in Greek literature outside the Bible in the 1st century BC. At this point I need to point out a piece of evidence, which seems to have been overlooked in this debate, which I believe changes the whole balance of the argument (I thank Andrew Chapman for bringing this to my attention). In **'The Sand Reckoner'** by **Archimedes** (287-212 BC) he clearly uses *apostasia* in a spatial sense, of physical distance or separation. This text reads: **"the circle in which the earth is supposed to revolve has the same ratio to the distance** (*apostasian*) **of the fixed stars as the centre of a sphere to its surface."** This has special importance as it is the very first use of the word *apostasia* in our possession, and it proves that the idea of physical separation was within the possible range of meanings of the word in the koine period (this is related to the idea of physical departure, which causes a separation). This first use of *apostasia* suggests that the basic physical sense was originally its primary meaning (like the verb), even if it later became a secondary use of the word. Thus its original simple meaning (like its root verb) is physical departure or separation, even if later it was often used to describe a religious separation, defection or rebellion.

*apostasia* is found 5 times in the LXX (the Greek Old Testament, 3rd/2nd century BC): Joshua 22:22 (rebellion); 2Chron 28:19, 29:19; 33:19 (unfaithfulness); Jer 2:19 (wickedness); 1Maccabees 2:15. It also occurs 7 times in Aquila (Deut 15:9; Judges 19:22; 1Kgdms 2:12; 10:27; 25:17; Proverbs 16:27;

Nahum 1:11), once in Theodotion (3Kgdms 21:13), and twice in Symmachus (1Kgdms 1:16; 2:12). In each of these instances, the meaning is religious or political defection. In addition there are a couple of papyrus fragments, quoted by Moulton and Milligan, where the word means 'a rebel.' This is evidence that the primary meaning of the word became a departure in a religious or political sense rather than a simple physical sense. However the relatively small number of these cases do not exclude the possibility that this word had a secondary sense of physical departure, and **the Archimedes quote, at about the same time as the LXX, establishes beyond doubt that a simple physical departure or separation is a possible meaning of this word.**

In the New Testament there is only one other time than in 2Thessalonians 2 that this noun is used and that is in <u>Acts 21:21</u> where Paul is accused of teaching Jews to depart from Moses: **"they have been informed about you that you teach all the Jews who are among the Gentiles to forsake** (*apostasia*) **Moses, saying that they ought not to circumcise their children nor to walk according to the customs."** Here the emphasis is on a spiritual departure, but it is Greek thinking to totally separate the spiritual from the physical (as if it were one or the other). In Hebrew thinking these two are closely connected, for a spiritual departure always results in a physical departure. In this case, spiritually departing from Moses would result in physically departing from the synagogue and not participating in the many physical customs, just as this verse points out. Thus the 'apostasia' in this verse includes a physical departure from the Jewish community as well as (resulting from) a spiritual departure from Moses. In any case, this one verse cannot possibly be used to limit the meaning of *apostasia* to a spiritual departure, and exclude the possibility of a physical departure.

**\*Later in the Patristic era,** there is no question that *apostasia* included the idea of physical departure within its range of meanings. **Jerome** (347 - 420 AD) chose to translate it into Latin as 'discessio', a word that means departure (usually in a physical sense), pointing to the fact that in his time, this meaning was understood to be part of the range of meanings of *apostasia*. Another example from the **6th century AD** is **Olympiodorus Meteorology. 320.2.**

**Lampe's Patristic Greek Lexicon also** gives an example of a spatial departure from a **5th century** New Testament apocryphal work: **'The Assumption of the Virgin.'** The amazing thing about this example is that in it *apostasia* is used to describe a physical translation or rapture! Sections 31–32 read: **"The Holy Ghost said to the apostles and the mother of the Lord: "Behold, the governor has sent a captain of a thousand against you, because the Jews have made a tumult. Go out therefore from Bethlehem, and fear not; for behold, I will bring you by a cloud to Jerusalem." The apostles therefore rose up straightaway and went out of the house, bearing the bed of their lady the mother of God, and went forward towards Jerusalem: and immediately, just as the Holy Ghost said, they were lifted up by a cloud and were found at Jerusalem in the house of their lady."** This clearly describes a 'rapture' of the apostles and Mary. Section 33 continues: **"But when the captain came to Bethlehem and did not find there the mother of the Lord, nor the apostles, he laid hold upon the Bethlehemites... For the captain did not know of the departure of the apostles and the mother of the Lord to Jerusalem."** This 'rapture' is now described as a 'departure', the Greek word being *apostasia*. Here is clear evidence that *apostasia* can refer to a 'rapture.'

Thus we have seen that in the Classical, the Koine and the Patristic eras, the times before, during and after the New Testament times, *apostasia* certainly included within its range of meanings the idea of spatial separation or physical departure, as well as a spiritual departure from the truth, and this is only to be expected considering that this is the basic and primary use of the verb from which it is derived. This is illustrated by fact that when Paul used the related verb in 1Timothy 4:1: "some shall **depart** from the faith", he had to qualify 'depart' by a phrase indicating that he was speaking of a spiritual departure, showing that the word itself did not inherently carry this meaning. Although Jewish literature in particular mostly came to use *apostasia* metaphorically to describe a spiritual departure from the truth, this does not justify eliminating its basic literal meaning. It is understandable, since the ideas of departure from the faith of Israel and rebellion against a foreign power were major themes of their literature at that time, that *apostasia* was used repeatedly in a religious sense in such contexts. But the word does not intrinsically carry the meaning of defection or revolt. In each biblical case it is only given that particular meaning by a qualifying phrase and/or by the context. We only know it has this meaning, because the context makes it clear. Thus as the Archimedes quote confirms these are acquired meanings of the word supplied by the context in which it is used, not its original, basic, literal meaning, and so should not be imposed on the word when the context does not point to such meanings, as in the case of its use in 2Thessalonians, where it has no qualifying phrase and the context does not refer to a religious defection, but to the Rapture.

This brings us back to my 2nd main contribution to this debate, the argument that unlike Greek thinking, which makes a strong separation between the spiritual and physical, the Hebrews saw the two as working closely together, as indeed they often do, and so would naturally have maintained both meanings in their use of the word, and even would have often seen both aspects together when used in a particular situation. It would have been unnatural to their way of thinking to sever off the physical meaning from the spiritual. This tendency is the result of Greek-type thinking that is better at dividing things into separate compartments (analysis), than holding them in synthesis, creating a bias towards 'either/or' thinking rather than 'both/and' thinking. I am saying this to correct the bias that presumes the word lost its original basic physical meaning, when the starting presumption should be the opposite, and indeed we have shown that the evidence from its usage in all eras bears this out, for although the primary use is religious, there are clear cases when it is used in a physical sense. Considering the relatively few uses of this noun in the surviving literature this is surely significant. The apparent lack of use of *apostasia* in referring to a physical departure in the koine period (except arguably 2Thess 2:3 itself) has convinced many against its application to the Rapture, especially as this is the time-period leading up to the New Testament. But **the Archimedes quote changes all that** as it shows the word was indeed used in a physical way at that time. Although Feinberg's database search revealed no instances when the word was used in a physical sense during this time, this is because he chose to search only from the 2nd century BC to the 1st century AD, thus missing the Archimedes quote, which was from just before his starting point.

Sadly this bias is manifested in overstating the case. House has to correct Gundry's claim that *apostasia* and its cognates occur over 40 times in the LXX and all carry the idea of political or religious defection. In fact there are over 220 occurrences, of which at least 66 express spatial separation, compared to religious defection (x 53) and political defection (x 8). If he meant to speak of the noun alone, he should not try and hide the relatively small number of usages by including the cognates in the total number quoted. Another example of this kind of smoke and mirrors is Feinberg's claim: *"If one searches for the uses of the noun 'apostasia' in the 355 occurrences of the 300 year period between the 2nd century BC and the 1st century AD, one will not find a single instance where this word refers to a physical departure."* In fact 355 is the number of occurrences of the noun and its cognates, and so if he is focusing on the use of the noun he should have used that number, which is a small fraction of 355, and so obviously far less impressive for his case. Moreover by limiting the range of years as he did he excluded the Archimedes quote, which invalidates his claim in any case.

This word, with its basic root meaning of a physical departure, but also often denoting a spiritual rejection, used by a Hebrew mind which naturally holds both physical and spiritual aspects together, makes *apostasia* the perfect word to describe the Rapture, and is no doubt the reason Paul chose it. For the Rapture is not just a simple physical event, it is also filled with great spiritual significance. Paul would not have been bound into the oversharp Greek-style separation of physical and spiritual and would have wanted a word that did not merely describe the Church's physical departure, but which also carried a sense of its spiritual significance, which would add depth to his explanation of its connection to the Day of the Lord. When we study the context of 2Thessalonians 2:3 we will see how perfectly *apostasia* does this. Thus Paul chose *apostasia*, because it lent itself to the fusion of both the spiritual and physical aspects of the Departure of the Church, for it can refer to a physical departure from a place, which has a spiritual significance (basis), or a spiritual rejection and rebellion against a system, which results in a physical withdrawal from it. This fusion perfectly describes the nature of the Rapture, which is a decisive departure and withdrawal of the Church from the earth, based on a rejection of the evil world-system, which is about to come under the judgment of the Day of the Lord. The Rapture is the Church departing from an evil world that is about to be judged, being separated from it, so that it does not share in its judgment, just as righteous Lot departed unrighteous Sodom, just before judgment fell. Paul was saying that they were not yet in the Day of the Lord (v2), for the Day of the Lord cannot come unless the *apostasia* comes first (v3). By using *apostasia* for the Rapture he was not just stating the fact of the Pre-Tribulation Rapture, but also explaining its necessity, for the true Church is identified with Christ and not with this world-system, in fact it has forsaken it and stands in opposition to it, and this spiritual reality will be manifested by her removal from it in the Rapture, when it comes time for Christ to judge this world, for it is not right for her to partake in its judgment.

Paul had made this very point in 1Thessalonians 5, when he discussed the timing of the Rapture (v1), saying that: **"the Day of the Lord** (Tribulation) **comes** (begins) **as a thief in the night** (the Rapture, Matthew 24:43)" (v2). He then defined 'the Day of the Lord' as the time of labour-pains and destruction (the Tribulation, Matthew 24:7,8) that will come upon the whole world (v3). He then explained why the Rapture of the Church must take place before this time of worldwide judgment: **"THEY** (the world) **shall not escape** (the destruction of the Day of the Lord). **BUT YOU, brethren, are not in darkness, so that this Day should overtake YOU as a thief. You are all sons of light and sons of the day. We are not of the night nor of darkness"** (v3-5). The Church is contrasted to the world in darkness, believers (the sons of light) do not belong to the darkness of this world-system, and so will not come under its judgment. We belong to the kingdom of light, whereas the world in darkness is under God's wrath, that will be released in the Day of the Lord. Since no one on earth will escape it, the Church must be removed from the earth before it starts. Therefore, because of the contrasting natures of the Church and the world, of light and darkness, they will have 2 very different destinies: **"For God has not appointed us to wrath** (the Day of the Lord), **but to obtain salvation** (in the Rapture) **by our Lord Jesus Christ"**(v8).

Therefore the physical event of the Pre-Tribulation Rapture is seen as a moral and spiritual imperative, that she will not share in the Day of the Lord

Judgment upon the world, because although she is in the world, she is not of it. She shines as a light in the darkness of this world. Thus the Rapture is a physical event that expresses her spiritual rejection of what it stands for. Her physical departure from the world and gathering to Jesus, is a manifestation of her previous spiritual departure from the darkness of this world, by coming to Jesus. The departure of the Church from the earth unto Jesus above, opens the way for Him to start the time of judgment, called 'the Day of the Lord' upon the earth.

This revelation of the spiritual basis for the Rapture explains why *apostasia* is the perfect word for God to have chosen in 2Thessalonians 2, as it fits the context perfectly, expressing and enriching the main thought. The opposition of the Church to the spirit of evil in the world is also confirmed in v6-8, where the Church (with the Holy Spirit) is described as the one restraining evil, so that only when it is removed (in the Rapture) can the antichrist be manifested and then judged (in the Day of the Lord). Finally, it is striking how similar this is to Jesus' instructions to His disciples on leaving a place that has rejected their witness to Him: **"Whoever will not receive you nor hear your words, when you depart from that house or city, shake off the dust from your feet"** (Matthew 10:14). Mark 6:11 and Luke 9:5 explain that this functions: **"as a testimony against them."** This was a sign that they were guilty and deserving of judgment for having rejected the message. So if having completed their witness it was rejected, they were to physically depart the place and spiritually disassociate themselves from any of its defilement, symbolised by shaking off its dust. This will ultimately be fulfilled at the Rapture. When the Church has completed its witness to the world, it will leave it and its dramatic and rapid departure will demonstrate its rejection of the world and all it stands for. This *apostasia* will be a sign to the world that judgment is about to fall, but God in His mercy will still give people a chance to repent, for this dramatic warning sign will be a wake up call to many, causing them to turn to Christ for forgiveness and salvation.

## CONTEXT

Having established that physical departure is within the semantic range of meanings of *apostasia*, we will now show that the context of 2Thessalonians 2 points clearly to the Rapture as the correct interpretation. The importance of context is magnified in this case, because 'the *apostasia*' in v3 has the definite article ('the') and no qualifier explaining its meaning. This combination only happens when what the word refers to is a definite event, which is so well-defined to the reader's mind that no qualifier is needed. Thus it must be obvious from the context. The only other case of *the apostasia* arising in this way is in 1Maccabees 2:15, and reading the preceding 46 verses makes it absolutely clear that it refers to a religious defection. This is why the term with the article needs no further qualification, even though it could potentially have a variety of possible meanings. Applying this same logic to *the apostasia* in 2Thessalonians, leads us to conclude that it must refer to a definite event whose nature is clear and well defined by the preceding context. On this basis we'll see the only valid candidate is the Rapture.

The meaning of this *apostasia* should be obvious from the prior context of 2Thessalonians 2:3, that is, 1Thessalonians and 2Thessalonians 1:1 - 2:2. That is, there should be a well defined end-time departure or defection discussed in this section of Scripture that corresponds to the *apostasia* of 2:3 in such a way that the readers would easily recognise it as such. There is nothing in these chapters corresponding to a religious defection or political rebellion. However, the single topic discussed more than any other in these chapters is the Departure of the Church in the Rapture. Almost every chapter in 1Thessalonians has a direct reference to it (1:9-10, 2:19, 4:13-18 which gives the most complete statement on the Rapture, and 5:1-11).

Finally and most importantly, the verses immediately before 2Thessalonians 2:3, which begin and introduce the passage under consideration, announce that the subject under discussion is the Rapture: **"Now, brethren, concerning the Coming of our Lord Jesus Christ and our gathering together to Him"** (v1). In this way, Paul emphasises his previous teaching on the Rapture in 1Thessalonians, causing us to remember it and focus upon it as we read what he has to say next on this subject. Thus it is the key to interpreting the following verses correctly. So in v3 when Paul refers to 'the Departure' without specifying what departure he was talking about, the law of interpretation says it must be obvious from the context, so we should ask: "Is there an obvious departure in the context which is marked so clearly that it was unnecessary for Paul to clarify any further what this Departure was?" The answer is a resounding 'Yes' - the Departure of the Church in v1, which is not only the declared subject of the passage, but the major topic of the Thessalonian epistles! Context determines meaning, so the fact *apostasia* is often used to mean religious defection in other kinds of contexts is irrelevant to this situation. In these other passages the context naturally points to a defection, but this is not the case in 2Thessalonians, where the context naturally points to the departure of the Church.

Alternative interpretations, which do not involve the Rapture, are not only inconsistent with the preceding context, but also with the rest of the passage in 2Thessalonians 2, for they have Paul announcing in v1 that the main subject under discussion is the Rapture, but then in their reading of the following verses the Rapture is never mentioned after that! Yet for those who have eyes to see the central theme is the Rapture and its relationship to antichrist and the Day of the Lord (which opens with the revelation of the antichrist). Thus following the law of context points strongly to the Rapture being the Departure in v3.

In v2 Paul explains the purpose of his teaching in this passage: **"we ask you not to be soon shaken in mind or troubled, either by spirit or by word or by letter, as if from us, as though the Day of the Lord had come."** The perfect tense of the verb 'to come' used here indicates that a false rumour had arisen that the Day of the Lord had already arrived and was present, and this was troubling the Thessalonians. Every use of the perfect tense of this verb agrees with this meaning, and there is no question that this is the correct translation. This fact confirms what we deduced about the Day of the Lord from 1Thess 5:2-3, namely that 'the Day of the Lord' here cannot be the 2nd Coming, for it would be plain to all that the Lord had not returned in glory. Neither could it be the Rapture for again it would be obvious to all that this had not happened, and so they would not have taken seriously any claims to that effect. Instead 'the Day of the Lord' must be the Tribulation, which is consistent with its Old Testament usage denoting a special time of judgment in the end-times. This also explains why they were disturbed, for they had been taught the Pre-Tribulation Rapture by Paul in 1Thessalonians and orally (v5), so when they were told that the Tribulation had overtaken them and they had not been raptured, so they will have to go through this terrible time of wrath, their reaction is understandable. The KJV translation: 'the Day of the Lord was at hand' is invalid and is driven by theological not grammatical reasons, for if you assume the Day of the Lord is the 2nd Coming, then the literal translation ('the Day of the Lord has already come') makes no sense. The literal statement only makes sense when you understand 'the Day of the Lord' is not the 2nd Coming.

In v3 Paul then explains why they could not possibly be in the Day of the Lord: **"Let no one deceive you by any means; for that Day will not come unless** *the apostasia* (departure) **comes first, and the man of sin is revealed."** We have established that the only candidate for this departure in the prior context is the Rapture of the Church. Moreover, when the passage is read from this viewpoint it makes perfect sense. Thus Paul is saying that the Tribulation will not start until the Departure of the Church comes first, and only then will the man of sin be revealed, that is, only then will the Tribulation begin (the revelation of antichrist happens at the start of the Tribulation - Daniel 9:27, Revelation 6:1-2). Thus Paul answers by reaffirming the Pre-Tribulation Rapture, that the Church must be removed before the Day of the Lord begins and antichrist is revealed. This is exactly the answer we would expect from Paul if he taught the Pre-Tribulation Rapture. To those claiming we are already in the Day of the Lord, the most obvious reply of a Pre-Tribber would be that we cannot possibly be in the Day of the Lord because the Rapture has not happened yet, and the antichrist has not been revealed, and that is exactly what Paul said. For a Pre-Tribber to interpret *apostasia* in any other way creates difficulties, for in that case Paul failed to make the obvious point that would have clearly settled the issue (that the Rapture must happen first), and instead he appealed to some specific but undefined apostasy that must happen first, which is not mentioned in Thessalonians, or in the rest of Scripture, but that the Thessalonian readers knew about from Paul's oral teaching. For this reason there are many theories about what this apostasy is, but we can't know it, so we can only speculate, and we cannot recognise it when it happens. This is unsatisfactory for it contradicts the sufficiency of Scripture, especially as this is an end-time sign needed most of all by the end-time generation.

Thus any Pre-Tribulation interpretation that does not see *apostasia* as the Rapture is unsatisfactory, and so it is disappointing that this interpretation has not yet been accepted widely in the Pre-Tribulation camp. The main reason has been the argument that 'physical departure' is not one of the viable meanings of *apostasia*. However, the evidence presented in this article shows that this is simply not so. Therefore, I appeal to my fellow Pre-Tribulationists to embrace the Rapture interpretation of *apostasia* in 2Thessalonians 2:3 as it makes perfect sense of the passage and agrees with the context, as well as being consistent with word usage. Furthermore, if *apostasia* speaks of a defection from the faith which must happen first, it is hard to understand why Paul would use it as a means of bringing comfort to the troubled believers, as he seeks to do in this chapter (v2,3,17), just as he does in 1Thessalonians 4:18 and 5:11 where the Rapture is the basis for comfort.

This view also has the advantage of harmonising v3 with v6-8, as they contain parallel thoughts, for in v3 the *apostasia* is followed by the revelation of the man of sin, and in v6-8 the taking away of the Restrainer is followed by the revelation of the lawless one: **"And now you know what is restraining, that he may be revealed in his own time. For the mystery of lawlessness is already at work; only He who now restrains will do so until He is taken out of the way. And then the lawless one will be revealed."**

If the *apostasia* is the Rapture every-thing fits perfectly. Having reminded them that the Departure of the Church from the world must happen before the antichrist is revealed to the world (v3), on the basis of this knowledge he expected them to know what was presently preventing and restraining his revelation (v6). Simple logic dictates that the 'WHAT is restraining' has to be the Church. But of course it is not the Church on its own, but the Holy Spirit indwelling the Church, so in v7 the description of the Restrainer shifts from 'WHAT' to 'HE who now restrains.' Thus the present Restrainer of the antichrist could be described as the Holy Spirit working with and through the Church, or as the Church empowered by the Spirit. Logically this restraining ministry will continue until the Restrainer is 'taken out of the way' in the Rapture (v7), and then this will allow the antichrist to be revealed (v8). Thus we can see how v6-8 repeat and develop the thought of v3. Having declared that the antichrist cannot be revealed until the Departure of the Church (v3), in v6-8 Paul explains the reason for this fact. It is because the Church, indwelt by God's Spirit, is presently holding back the antichrist from being revealed and will continue to do so until its Departure from the world, so that only when it is taken out of his way (by its removal in the Rapture) will satan be able to manifest the antichrist to the world.

Whereas in alternative interpretations both the *apostasia* and the identity of *the Restrainer* are left undefined by the context and so become a matter of speculation, this interpretation allows *the apostasia* to be defined by the context, which in turn allows us to determine the identity of *the Restrainer* from the context. Thus it brings harmony and coherence to the whole passage, whereas other interpretations are left with a collection of undefined and unconnected ideas. Thus this literal interpretation of *apostasia* harmonises the whole passage with its context and central theme and solves all its problems. It's the only interpretation that explains why Paul was able to just call it *the apostasia* without adding any explanation. He clearly expected them to know what he was talking about, so it must be clear from the prior context, and the only 'departure' in the prior context is the Rapture. Moreover this literal interpretation transforms 2Thessalonians 2 from a passage that can be harmonised with the Pre-Tribulation Rapture to a passage that plainly declares it, in fact it is the main point of the passage. Thus Pre-Tribulationists should embrace it, not resist it.

In response to the question as to whether there is a single passage of the Bible that reveals the 2 phases of Christ's Return (Rapture and 2nd Coming) separated by the Tribulation, we reply that 2Thessalonians 2 is one such passage. The Rapture (His initial coming to the air for His saints) is in v1 ('our gathering together to Him'), and His 2nd Coming to the earth to destroy antichrist and establish His Kingdom here is in v8. The coming of antichrist during the Tribulation is clearly located between the 2 phases of Christ's Return (his activity is described in v3-12). Thus a straightforward reading of this passage demonstrates the Pre-Tribulation view. If in addition *the apostasia* is recognised to be the Rapture, then v3 is a plain statement of this view, which is then reinforced further by the further explanation of the Restrainer in v6-8.

In closing, I want to answer a couple of possible objections. There is a Post-Tribulationist interpretation that claims *the apostasia* is the rebellion of antichrist described in the later verses, and so is in the context.

This must be rejected for 2 reasons: (1) Common sense dictates that the assumed knowledge of v3 must come from what has previously been said in the verses before it. Paul expects the reader of v3 to understand what he means, because he has already discussed it, not because he will explain it later. A basic principle of good communication is to define your terms first so people know what you are talking about. (2) This interpretation of v3 says the Day of the Lord cannot come unless the *apostasia* (rebellion of antichrist) happens first, and (thus) the man of sin is revealed. This then requires the Day of the Lord to be the 2nd Coming of Christ, which makes a nonsense of verse 2, which describes what occasioned Paul's discussion. The Thessalonians were disturbed because they thought the Day of the Lord had come, and Paul had to explain to them why it had not. If they understood the Day of the Lord was His glorious Return this would be nonsensical, as it was obvious He had not returned. Also if the Day of the Lord had suddenly come upon them in some way, then they would not have been 'troubled', but rather they would have been rejoicing, for their rapture and gathering together to Christ (to be with Him forever) was now imminent. The only way to make sense of v2 is that the Day of the Lord is an extended period of judgment, from which the Church is promised deliverance by Rapture, so those who thought they might already be in it were naturally troubled. In this case, the rebellion of antichrist is an event within the Day of the Lord, and so it cannot be the *apostasia* of v3, which must take place BEFORE the Day of the Lord.

Another technical issue is the implication of the word FIRST in v3: **"that Day (of the Lord) will not come unless *the apostasia* comes FIRST, and the man of sin is revealed."** Does it mean that the Day of the Lord will not come until BOTH *the apostasia* and the revelation of the man of sin has taken place? Or does it mean that the Day of the Lord will not come until the *apostasia* comes first, and then the man of sin will be revealed (as the key event at the start of the Day of the Lord)? Both interprctations are grammatically possible, but other prophetic scriptures tell us that the revelation of the antichrist takes place at the start of the Day of the Lord (Revelation 6:1-2, Daniel 9:27). In fact, it is the definitive event on earth that marks the start of the Tribulation. Therefore the latter view must be correct. Paul assumes that they understood that the Day of the Lord is the time when the antichrist comes to power, which was why they were troubled at the thought that they were in that time, so he was saying this time won't come unless the Rapture comes first, and then the antichrist will be revealed, which is equivalent to describing the start of the Day of the Lord.

One can discern 2 clear points in v3: (1) the *apostasia* comes before the Day of the Lord (from the first part of the verse), (2) the *apostasia* comes before the revelation of antichrist (from the 2nd part of the verse). It does not necessarily say that the revelation of antichrist comes before the Day of the Lord (Tribulation), and this would contradict other scriptures. Clearly it makes better sense as a parallelism, where the coming of the Day of the Lord is equivalent to the manifestation of antichrist. Since there are 2 main aspects of the Tribulation that would trouble anyone: (1) it is a time of Divine Wrath (the Day of the Lord), and (2) it is the time of the antichrist's manifestation as ruler, in v3 Paul gave a 2-fold assurance, comforting them that they were not in this time, for *the apostasia* had not yet happened. This is then confirmed in v6-12, which say that the Church (Restrainer) must be removed (in the Rapture) before the antichrist is revealed and deceives the world in the Tribulation until Christ returns to destroy him.

# *Appendix 2 – The 4 Schools of Prophetic Interpretation

**\*1. The PRETERIST** School believes that most (if not all) prophecies (especially the Olivet Discourse and Revelation, as well as the Old Testament prophecies about the judgments of 'the Day of the Lord') have already been fulfilled in the events surrounding the destruction of Jerusalem by the Romans in AD 70! Unbelievably they believe that this fulfilled the prophecies of Christ coming in power and glory. They believe the references to the last days or end times, characterised by apostasy, refer to the last days of Israel's Age of favour (AD 33-70), after which the earth entered a new phase of history, with the Church forever replacing Israel as God's people. Thus these prophecies were written for the first century Christians to prepare them for what was shortly going to happen (the candidates for antichrist being the Roman Caesar Nero and the false Jewish Messiah's of that time), so these prophecies have little relevance for us today as they have already been fulfilled.

However, anyone adopting literal interpretation has to reject this approach for it is clear that these prophecies have not come to pass yet in any literal sense. Sadly most seem to feel free to abandon literal interpretation whenever necessary into order to promote their vision of what they think the future should be, rather than accepting God's revelation at face value. The Preterists are especially guilty of this tendency. Also Preterism requires Revelation to have been written before AD 70, but all the best historical evidence points to the fact it was written during the reign of the Roman Emperor Domitian, in about AD 95, which proves that it is false (see 'Dominion Theology: Blessing or Curse?' by Wayne House/Thomas Ice).

Preterism finds its main basis in <u>Matthew 24:34</u>: **"Assuredly, I say to you, this generation will by no means pass away till all these things take place."** They assume that 'this generation' is the generation to which Jesus is speaking, but the context, which describes the Signs leading up to the 2nd Coming, indicates that Jesus is speaking about the end-time generation that sees the beginning of these Signs. Preterism comes in 2 forms. Full Preterism says that the destruction of Jerusalem fulfilled all end time prophecies, including the resurrection of the dead, Jesus' 2nd Coming, and the Final Judgment. Partial Preterists realise that the consequence of following this system of interpretation leads to heresy and so modify it and call themselves Orthodox Preterists. They believe there are prophecies yet to be fulfilled by the Return of Christ and a future resurrection and judgment. Once people become partial Preterists there is a tendency to go all the way into full Preterism because it is the more logically consistent version.

The Olivet Discourse consists of Jesus' answer to the 3 questions of Matthew 24:3 about the signs of the destruction of the Temple, the 2nd Coming, and the end of the world (or age). The Full Preterists say that these must have all been fulfilled by AD 70 because of v34 ('the end' being the end of the Jewish age). But even though it is the logical consequence of their position, the partial preterists step back from the brink of saying that the Bible does not reveal the 2nd Coming of Christ and the Final Judgment, by admitting that parts of Matthew 24 and Revelation do prophesy events that are yet to take place at the end of time, which will be initiated by the literal Return of Jesus. Although full Preterists often try to maintain their orthodoxy by affirming their faith in the Return of Christ and the Final Judgment based on the historic Creeds of the Church, this requires them to reject 'Sola Scripture' (the sufficiency of Scripture) which is foundational to our faith, the rejection of which leads to even greater heresies (Revelation 22:18-19).

A literal approach to the Olivet Discourse is that Jesus' prophetic answer to the 1st question about the destruction of the Temple (recorded in Luke 21:20-24) was fulfilled in AD 66-70), but His answer to the other questions concerning the End of the Age (Tribulation) and the 2nd Coming, have clearly not yet been fulfilled. What could possibly have motivated this unnatural reading of scripture? It originated from a Roman Catholic scholar who realised the Protestant Reformers were making effective use of Revelation in proving the Roman Church was apostate, fulfilling the prophecies of 'the woman riding the beast' in Revelation 17, with the Pope being an antichrist ('vicar of Christ' literally means 'in the place of Christ', which is a possible meaning of anti-christ). So he was motivated to create an alternative way of interpreting Revelation and the other prophetic scriptures. Another hint as to its dark origins is the way it could be used as a basis for anti-semitism as it denies any future for Israel in God's Plan.

Preterism also appeals to those who want to promote Dominion Theology, because a normal reading of the Bible's Eschatology contradicts their vision of the Church taking over the world. They want to have what they would call a 'victorious eschatology' (as if the glorious truth is not victorious enough - of Christ returning for us as the Bridegroom coming for His Bride, then judging and cleansing the world of all evil and establishing His Kingdom of righteousness, joy and peace on earth). Not content to stay with Christ's marching orders by fulfilling the Great Commission by evangelism and discipleship, they go beyond this by saying that we also have a dominion mandate, which requires us to Christianise the world, transform society, taking over the culture, taking our cities for God (not so much saving the people, but changing the institutions). Such a vision is certainly optimistic and appeals to man's desire for outward success and power. But Dominion Theology has dangers, as discussed in Appendix 5. Its main problem is that it has no clear scriptural support, which is strange for something so important. Moreover the idea of the Church increasingly taking dominion over the world-system, so that Christ is held in Heaven waiting to return when the Church has put all things under His feet, plainly contradicts the scriptural description of the future, which reveals apostasy in the Church and the whole world lying under the power of satan throughout this present Age (2Cor 4:4, Eph 2:2, 1John 5:19). Also this Age will end with the Tribulation, a time when evil comes to its fullness and becomes dominant, with the whole world being ruled by the antichrist. Therefore, the kingdoms of this world will only become the Kingdom of our God through the intervention of King Jesus, who will personally establish His Kingdom on earth at His Return. But Partial Preterism says that all these 'negative' prophecies have been fulfilled, allowing the dominionist to believe that things are going to get better and better as God's Kingdom is advanced through the Church until she has taken over all the systems of the world for God. This view is overly optimistic as the Lord has never authorised the Church to do this. Moreover, it is dangerous for it means the Church will not be on guard against the increasing apostasy in the end-times, and it will relax its hold on the Gospel in order (1) to unite with other religious groups in its attempts to maximise its power to change the world, and (2) be less offensive to the world in its attempt to gain a greater position in it.

Doctrine is not determined by us choosing the most optimistic view possible but by being true to what Scripture actually says. The Biblical view of the end-times is realistic, containing both optimistic and realistic elements. It is victorious because it reveals Christ's total and final victory over the powers of evil, but neither does it deny the power and growth of evil in this world. Also in it the glory rightly belongs to Christ, not to the Church. On the one hand, the world and the apostate church that denies the Gospel will get darker and darker until God judges them in the Tribulation and 2nd Coming. On the other hand, there are Biblical grounds for optimism that the true Church will get brighter and brighter as it holds forth the Gospel and brings in a great soul-harvest from all the nations, thus fulfilling her real mission (the Great Commission) before Christ establishes His Kingdom, when His saints will reign with Him (Mark 13:10, James 5:7, Revelation 5:9,10, Romans 11:25). Often this issue is presented as a choice between an overly pessimistic view of the Church failing and becoming totally apostate and an overly optimistic view of the Church taking over and driving satan off the planet. The present and future realities are more complex. Apostasy within the church and evil in the world will continue to grow, but that is not the whole story. At the same time God will fulfil the Purpose of the Church Age, by calling out many from every nation to belong to Him through the Gospel. There is every hope for revival, and the pattern of earthly harvests (after the former and latter rains) give good reason for hope that the last days of the Church Age will see the true Church having great success in fulfilling her mission to bring in a great soul harvest. Indeed this is happening now for the worldwide Church has been growing rapidly over the last 100 years as it's faithful to spread the Gospel. The imminence of the Rapture is preserved, because only God knows when the full measure of the harvest of the nations (the fullness of the Gentiles) will be gathered in. Sadly many following a Dominionist vision will compromise the Gospel to gain power in this world and establish a working unity with other groups, and will end up as part of the apostate church in the darkness, for without the Power of the Gospel we have nothing to offer this world (Romans 1:16-17). Thus what has taken place over the last century, the parallel growth of the light of the Gospel and the darkness of sin and religious deception, will continue until the End of the Age.

Thus we see that the correct Eschatology keeps us focused on our heavenly hope and our God-given earthly mission to reach people with the Gospel and so gather the precious fruit of the earth, whereas a false Eschatology diverts our energies to fulfil an futile earthly hope of establishing the Kingdom now, so that after we have spent all our time and energy in our 'kingdom building' we have little left to do what we are actually called to do. Those who like to call themselves apostles and prophets should make sure they are building on the foundation already established by the Biblical apostles and prophets (Ephesians 2:20), as recorded in

Scripture, rather than presenting visions that are created in their own imaginations as to what a victorious Church-Age should look like.

Another danger of the Preterist or Dominionist view is that it effectively creates a new dispensation after AD 70, so that much of what the apostles wrote before that time no longer applies today. For example, the warnings about apostasy and the man of sin and the end-time events. Also they claim that satan has now been fully dethroned from his place of authority over the world-system (Rev 12), so that the way is clear to the Church to take dominion and displace him and his principalities and powers. Thus the scriptures given to the apostles for their Age, which focus on a humble ministry of preaching the Gospel, being ready to face persecution from a hostile world ruled by satan, no longer apply today.

Moreover it follows that these scriptures are inadequate for our present Age when the 'glorious church' is being called to rise up and take dominion in the earth, the manifestation of the sons of God. New revelations are therefore needed for the Church, especially in the areas of prayer, spiritual warfare and taking dominion, and these are being provided by the new apostles and prophets who increasingly claim a status comparable to the foundational apostles and prophets, because they see themselves as laying the foundation for the future Church which will operate on a higher level than the early church. These new theologies and methods do not come from Scripture, but from the authority of these false apostles and prophets. Beware those who teach from their own thought and make only passing references to Scripture when it fits their ideas! There are true apostles and prophets today but they do not have the authority to add to Scripture, which is now complete and sufficient for us. Therefore any teaching that is not based in Scripture has little value, and distracts us from what is really important. It is not enough for them to say that no new revelation from God is allowed to contradict Scripture, for this is exactly what the Roman Church and all other cults do when they add their new relations (traditions) to the Bible. The result is always that the group follows the exciting new and now revelation and increasingly depart from the Bible.

Church history sadly confirms these facts. Whenever the Church adds to Scripture it goes into error and ends up with a false Gospel. Moreover, whenever the Church has pursued and gained political power (as with the Medieval Roman Church) its lust for power causes it to become compromised and corrupted. It becomes an oppressor denying religious liberty and ends up persecuting the true believers. Through these deceptions satan has greatly hindered the preaching of the Gospel and the salvation of the lost. Also those who submit to the power of the Church are led to believe that in so doing they are citizens of heaven, but this is a deception for salvation is only through the means of the Gospel. Moreover, modern charismatic attempts to take cities for God have signally failed despite great efforts at unbiblical dominionist spiritual warfare, whereas the church has made great strides forward wherever it is faithful to the Great Commission.

**\*2. The HISTORICIST** School seeks to make Revelation 6-19 more relevant by saying its predictions cover the whole Church Age. Thus it equates the current Church-Age with the Tribulation, and relates the Seal, Trumpet and Bowl Judgments to major historical events (usually centred on European history). It gives a symbolic coded prophecy of the Church Age, so it sees the Book of Revelation as tracing the course of the last 2,000 years. It has been the standard Protestant approach from the Reformation until 200 years ago, when many returned to a more literal view. It is the view of 7th Day Adventists, Mormons, and Jehovah Witnesses. It was used to equate the Roman Catholic institution and popes with the antichrist, and some use it to identify America as Babylon. Again this is an allegorical approach requiring a non-literal interpretation of prophecy.

**\*3. The FUTURIST** School (which is expounded in this book) is based on taking prophecy literally (using the same rules of interpretation as other areas of doctrine). That is, we take it in its plain meaning, according to the laws of language. If the literal meaning makes sense, then read it that way. Applying this principle it is clear that Revelation 4-22 has not yet been fulfilled; it still awaits a future fulfilment. Most end-time Bible Prophecy describes the future climax of the battle between good and evil. In this way, we don't have to make forced interpretations of prophecies in trying to show that they have already been fulfilled.

One criticism of FUTURISM is that the prophecies do not apply to us today, so studying prophecy has little value for us. But this is short-sighted. The same argument could be used to say it is pointless to study Bible history, as Prophecy is just His-story that has not happened yet! By revealing what God will do, we discover more about His character, power and purposes, and how we fit into the scheme of things and how we are to focus our lives and what purposes we should give ourselves to. Understanding the times in which we live and what lies ahead

Printed in Great Britain
by Amazon

42517339R00090